BRAND WARFARE

10 RULES FOR BUILDING THE KILLER BRAND

Lessons for New and Old Economy Players

DAVID F. D'ALESSANDRO

with Michele Owens

McGraw-Hill

New York   Chicago   San Francisco   Lisbon   London
Madrid   Mexico City   Milan   New Delhi   San Juan
Seoul   Singapore   Sydney   Toronto

McGraw-Hill

A Division of *The McGraw-Hill Companies*

3 4 5 6 7 8 9 0   DOC/DOC   0 9 8 7 6 5 4 3 2 1

ISBN 0-07-136293-2

This publication is designed to provide accurate and authoritative information in regard to the subject matter covered. It is sold with the understanding that the publisher is not engaged in rendering legal, accounting, or other professional service. If legal advice or other expert assistance is required, the services of a competent professional person should be sought.

—From a declaration of principles jointly adopted by a committee of
the American Bar Association and a committee of publishers.

Printed and bound by R. R. Donnelley & Sons Company.

McGraw-Hill books are available at special quantity discounts to use as premiums and sales promotions, or for use in corporate training programs. For more information, please write to the Director of Special Sales, Professional Publishing, McGraw-Hill, Two Penn Plaza, New York, NY 10121-2298. Or contact your local bookstore.

For Michael, Andrew, and Robert

CONTENTS

INTRODUCTION

O ne of the best lessons I ever learned in business, I learned
from one of my first public relations clients. Although I was
just a kid out of college, I was working at a big New York City public relations firm and feeling pretty wise in the ways of the world.
The client, on the other hand, was this little old guy from the
Midwest with a bow tie, a center-parted hairdo that hadn't been
seen since Alfalfa left "The Little Rascals," and the preposterous
name of Orville Redenbacher. The Chicago office of my firm sent
him to us to help him promote his product in the East, and one
day he showed up in our offices in the big city to tell us why his
gourmet popcorn would revolutionize the popcorn industry.

First of all, it was news to us that popcorn was an industry.
At the time, there were only two ways to buy popcorn to prepare
at home: the generic in bags and Jiffy Pop, a brand that was free
of all gourmet tendencies. "As much fun to *make* as it is to eat"
was the idea there.

Then Orville went on to explain *in minute detail* why the
hybrid corn he had developed was better, how his kernels popped
up almost twice as big, and how he personally guaranteed that
almost all of them would pop. To say that Orville took his popcorn

seriously was a severe understatement. He'd tell us conspiratorially, "Don't you hate it when the husks get caught in your teeth? Well, that's not going to happen as much with my corn. The husk is thinner." He anthropomorphized every kernel to the extent that the ones that refused to pop he called "the old maids." We thought he was insane. We literally thought he was insane.

Certifiable or not, however, his money was good, and we were his as long as his checks remained good. He clearly had his own game plan and would not be dissuaded from it. I remember someone at our firm trying to convince him to call his product the "100-Percent Better Popcorn." No, Orville said, they'd started out with a different name, but now he liked having his name on the jar.

Orville didn't spend a lot of money on advertising. He needed a public relations firm to get him some attention, so we threw a big party in New York City for hundreds of food editors. We weren't fools—we made sure the liquor was free flowing and managed to get everybody smashed. At a certain point in the evening, we trotted Orville out in his little bow tie, and he made a little speech about how every kernel of his corn pops.

To our amazement, all those jaded and allegedly sophisticated New York food critics found the concept amusing. Suddenly, every newspaper and magazine in America was writing about Orville's obsessive search for the world's best popping corn. Not only that, but supermarkets and consumers signed on to the idea, too. It was the start of a whole new life for Orville Redenbacher, who became a pop-culture icon and sold the business a few years later to Hunt-Wesson for a considerable sum of money.

If this were a Hollywood movie, I would now say that this admirable old man opened my young eyes to one inspiring truth: Quality always wins in the marketplace. But actually, that was *not* the lesson I took out of this experience. My apologies, Orville, but I've always suspected that the incredibly precise instructions you gave for popping it were as important to your superior popcorn as the stuff you put in the jar.

The real lesson Orville taught me was the power of a good brand to trump all rhyme or reason in the marketplace. Consumers were willing to pay a huge premium for his popcorn, not, in my opinion, because the product features were so startlingly different, and certainly not because they were saving money over the generic brand by eliminating the "old maids" that wouldn't pop. Instead, they bought Orville's popcorn because they found Orville endearing.

What Orville Redenbacher did is the absolute definition of branding: He took what had been a commodity nobody thought twice about and gave it a voice. He convinced consumers his corn was worth more because, unlike its competitors, it had a personality. In the process, he created an industry out of nothing, just as he had told me he would.

The lesson was not wasted on me when, in 1984, I went to work for John Hancock Financial Services. The bulk of our business back then was a very old-fashioned product, life insurance, with one extremely new-fashioned aspect: The product itself is vaporware, as insubstantial as any service peddled by the airiest dot-com company today. The only thing the consumer is buying when he or she buys life insurance is the company's promise that it will pay up if it's ever necessary. And the only thing life insurers are selling is their reputation, because if consumers cannot trust the quality of that promise, better prices or better product features mean nothing. (This is particularly true because you have to *die* in order to trigger those product features.)

If ever there were a brand-based business, life insurance is it. But most life insurance companies, which tend to be run by number crunchers, fail to comprehend this essential truth. The management of John Hancock, however, was smarter. When I came to John Hancock as head of communications, my assignment was to take its sleepy old brand and turn it into something as appealing to consumers in its own way as Orville's bow tie. And management and our board, fortunately, gave me plenty of support.

Fifteen years later, we wound up on the *New York Times'* list of the 100 best brands of the 20th century. More important, a strong brand enabled us to outsell our competitors and to convince a generation of consumers that prefers investments to life insurance that we are an excellent place to buy investment products, as well.

Of course, there is nothing original in my understanding that brand counts. By now, most American businesses have figured out that consumers like strong brands better than weak ones. In fact, two factors have led in recent years to a kind of brand mania in American business. The first is the widespread realization that investors are willing to pay a serious premium for the stocks of the most popular brands. The brand consultancy company Interbrand ranks the world's most valuable brands each year and calculates the value of these brands as a percentage of market capitalization. In the case of 2000's number-one brand, Coca-Cola, more than half the company's value—51 percent, or some $72.5 billion—is attributed to the brand.

The second factor encouraging brand mania is the incredible volatility that the Internet has contributed to the business landscape, as some of the dot-com brands have became towering giants overnight and some established brands have found themselves knocked to their knees equally abruptly. Taking a page out of the Amazon.com playbook, the startups of the great Internet surge of the late 1990s routinely fought first to establish themselves in consumers' consciousness and only second to make their businesses profitable. And, in the short term at least, this was not necessarily a stupid strategy.

Brand mania is by no means limited to business, either. More than any other business concept of the day, the idea of "brand" has infiltrated the culture. A movie star like Tom Hanks now talks openly about the importance of protecting the Tom Hanks brand. The State of Vermont thinks it's a brand, too, and is developing regulations to stop out-of-state companies from falsely appropriating the "Vermont" cachet. When the *New York Times* asked the official exorcist of the Cathedral of Notre Dame a few years ago why he was drawing customers from all over France when they could be exorcised just as well at their local churches, Father Claude Nicolas answered this way: "Evidently, they think Notre Dame is better. Of course, it has a certain brand name."

To say, then, to any group of professionals anywhere in the world that brand counts is to preach to the converted. So why bother to write a book about branding? Here's why: While the importance of a strong brand is widely understood, *nothing* is as misunderstood in American business as the question of how to use it.

Billions of dollars are squandered every year in the name of the brand. Businesses routinely milk their brands without investing in them, extend their brands without asking consumers what they think of the idea, buy up valuable brands in "merge-and-purge" binges, and then throw the brand names away in favor of corporate control.

Brand decisions are often treated as merely questions of advertising. But the stakes are much higher than that. Sears' move into the financial services business in the 1980s is a typical brand decision in that it determined how enormous amounts of capital, distribution, products, technology, and people were going to be used. Unfortunately for Sears, it turned out that consumers were not particularly interested in buying stocks from a store they associated with wrenches and undershirts.

Even some of the brand geniuses of the 1990s—companies like Nike and Coca-Cola that have been extraordinarily focused on keeping their logos swimming in front of consumers' eyes—have stumbled occasionally out of the failure to recognize one essential principle of branding: Brand is everything, the stuff you want to communicate to consumers and the stuff you communicate *despite* yourself.

By definition, "brand" is whatever the consumer thinks of when he or she hears your company's name. Thanks to the information revolution, "whatever" now includes labor practices, quality controls, environmental record, customer service, and every rumor that wings its way around the Internet. Nike is a prime example of a company whose brand has been affected by an issue that has nothing to do with marketing, namely, the working conditions in the third-world factories where Nike products are made. In a 1996 *BusinessWeek* story, when asked about the way the company's Indonesian subcontractors treat their workers, Nike Chairman Phil Knight said, "There's some things we can control and some things we can't control." That might have been true from a legal and practical standpoint, but from a brand standpoint, well, a corporation had better try to control *everything*, because there is nothing a brand cannot be held responsible for. Indeed, Nike suffered a relentless press pile-on over the labor issue and in 1998, Knight assessed the damage with refreshing honesty: "The Nike product," he said, "has become synonymous with slave wages, forced overtime, and arbitrary abuse."

Since everything a corporation does reflects on the brand, for better or for worse, every decision a corporation makes—whether to cut back on customer service, to expand into new markets, or to indulge the CEO's jock self-image by sponsoring a sports team—ought to be filtered through the prism of the brand. But too often, the brand is treated instead as an afterthought and ignored until it is in trouble. Why? Because, despite the lip service given to the concept of branding, the entire infrastructure of most corporations is hostile to brand building.

The truth is that even the best American corporations tend to be *full* of people who actually think they are doing their job by keeping the brand down. There are the lawyers who slow down a company's response in a crisis because they believe that short-term liability concerns ought to trump long-term brand considerations. There are the clerks who allow scandals to brew because they feel they have little to gain by reporting the dicey things they uncover. There are the financial types who allow good brands to atrophy because they resent the dollars it takes to build a brand. And there are the advertising managers who spend millions on campaigns that mean nothing to consumers because they fail to understand that the brand ought to drive the advertising and not the other way around.

As a result, most brand builders have to wage two wars at once: They have to beat competing brands into submission, at the same time as they hack through the corporate kudzu within their own organizations. By "brand builder," I mean anyone who is in any degree responsible for the care and feeding of a brand, from the enlightened CEO to the neophyte in the public relations department. To be a brand builder within a corporation is to risk being considered something less than a serious business player, because you will constantly be advocating that money be spent on what many people consider vaporous goals, such as establishing a voice and winning the goodwill of consumers. Whether you are the CEO or the new hire in marketing, it means constantly fighting the great skeptical "harrumph."

I wrote this book to help the brand builder win on all fronts, internal and external. It is not easy to build a great brand. It takes leadership to persuade the rest of the company to follow your vision. It takes an artistic sense of proportion and timing. It takes a ruthless willingness to distinguish yourself from competing brands and, hopefully, bury them in the process. It also takes a certain empathy with the people who buy your products and with humanity at large. To be a great brand builder takes some qualities that probably cannot be taught.

But whether you're a new economy player or an old economy behemoth, there are a handful of rules that can help you win the game. This book intends to lay them out.

ACKNOWLEDGMENTS

Many people promise to "someday write their own book." I still hope to do so . . . someday.

This book, though, is the result of relentless hard work on the part of many, many talented people. I had the opportunity to recount stories, offer advice, and opine about branding.

I would like to thank everyone who worked on the book and especially the following: Michele Owens, an extraordinarily talented writer whose credits include speeches for Mario Cuomo and Bill Weld in addition to screenplays. She patiently listened to me for over a year. She translated, interpreted, fact-checked, and wrote this story. She captured my thoughts and my voice. Becky Collet, a lawyer by training and a corporate communications professional, poked and prodded me every inch of the way. Her dedication to every page, word, and nuance is much appreciated. Steve Burgay is also an attorney and a senior vice president at John Hancock—I thank him not only for his editing ability, but also for coming up with the book idea and selling me on it. Jo Breiner, a talented researcher, dedicated many hours to getting the facts right. Jim Marchetti, yet another lawyer, pored over every sentence to make certain that the book not only was correct, but also that it made sense.

I am also very grateful to my wife Jeannette D'Alessandro for her advice, encouragement, and editing. Throughout this long process, she was always there with a gentle reminder that it would all be worth it in the end. Let's hope she's right.

Thanks also to Mary Glenn, my editor, and Chris Calhoun, my agent, for all their help.

Finally, I would like to thank the thousands of people I have met, under both traditional and bizarre circumstances, who collectively gave me the knowledge that I am able to pass on through *Brand Warfare*.

DAVID F. D'ALESSANDRO

BRAND WARFARE
10 RULES FOR BUILDING
THE KILLER BRAND

1

IT'S THE BRAND, STUPID

James Carville, Bill Clinton's brilliant political strategist in the watershed election of 1992, famously kept the campaign on track by scratching three little words on a dry-erase board near his desk: "The economy, stupid."

I've often thought CEOs should be forced to do exactly the same thing: take down the office Monet and, instead, put a thumbtack into a scrap of paper that says, "The brand, stupid."

The recent history of American business is littered with the corpses of executives who forgot that. And a huge number of these executives, by the way, were running companies with very big brands. The problem is that there's a tremendous arrogance that comes from having a big brand, and that arrogance makes it easy to forget that even the biggest brand only stays big at the pleasure of the consumers.

BRAND ARROGANCE WAS ONCE COMMONPLACE

The most incredible example of brand arrogance I ever witnessed personally was at Citibank, where I worked for seven or eight surreal months during the late 1970s. Of course, today Citigroup is one of the biggest and best financial services companies in the world. And back then, it was one of the world's finest banks, except for the division I worked in, which was a lunatic asylum.

Somebody came up with the bright idea that because this was Citibank, all the nation's smaller banks and credit unions were eager to emulate the company in any way possible. And the particular set of geniuses employed by this division sat around thinking about what they could sell to the smaller banks: computer systems, tapes on how to train tellers, prepackaged loan programs—you name it.

No product was too small or trivial. Our bosses would come in and say, "We're doing these Christmas calendars for Citibank, and you know, we can sell these calendars," as if Wachovia Bank were going to buy a Christmas calendar produced by the competition. It was seldom about the quality of the products or services we were offering; it was just about how much of the company's operating costs we could offset by pushing these things off onto smaller players. And the attitude of everybody involved was, "They will buy because it's *us*."

One meeting in particular opened my eyes to the future of this endeavor. We sat in a conference room while various technical people made presentations about the products that we were going to sell. That morning, one of the company's senior people graced us with his presence. Let's call him "The Executive." Of course, he would never leap down two or three rungs on the ladder to address the person presenting personally. As far as The Executive was concerned, assistant vice presidents like me were nonexistent. He would speak only to our boss.

That day, one of my unfortunate peers happened to be making a presentation about the sales of computer systems to correspondent banks, and he started to say things such as, "There are some limitations to getting this done," "The product has a limitation," and "There's a time-frame lag."

After a few minutes, The Executive bestirred himself to say to our boss, "Put the cup up."

I had no idea what The Executive was talking about. Our boss whispered something to somebody, who produced a Styrofoam coffee cup and set it on the table in front of the poor guy doing the presentation. Then our boss explained to the guy that every time he said something The Executive didn't like, he had to put a nickel in the cup.

What The Executive didn't like soon became abundantly clear. He refused to hear anything that in any way, shape, manner, or form took him off his timetable and delayed the launching of the product. And every time he did hear something that suggested the product was not yet ready for market, he'd hold up one finger and indicate that it was time for the peon irritating him to toss a nickel in the cup.

My colleague had a couple of nickels on him, but that was it. Watching him root around in his pockets looking for change was just painful. So finally, our boss put a $5 bill in the debit cup for him so he could finish his presentation.

I was thunderstruck by the whole scene. Despite the childishness of what was unfolding, the project that my colleague was trying to tell the truth about was a rather significant one that was costing millions and millions of dollars. And it was not just that The Executive—this arrogant shell of a professional manager—was humiliating someone who seemed to me far more honest and competent than he was. It was also what he said at the end of the meeting: "We're Citibank. This is a marketing problem, not a product problem."

In other words, because we were Citibank, and so obviously bigger and better than every other player, the quality of what we were selling didn't matter. We just needed to market it.

Though he was considered rather brilliant otherwise, The Executive misunderstood completely what it meant to have a strong brand. The presenter, on the other hand, had it right. We had to work harder and be better than anyone else simply *because* we were Citibank and had a reputation to uphold. Add in the fact that the smaller banks, the intended market for these products, were already suspicious that Citibank wanted to take them over, and there was simply no way we could sell those banks *anything* if our products were not so superior that they felt they couldn't live without them.

My colleague, of course, quit soon after, unwilling to work for an organization that would allow him to be publicly embarrassed just for doing his job. The meeting convinced me, too, that the division was going to fail, and I'd better exit. Sure enough, it cost Citibank hundreds of millions of dollars to watch this little notion implode. Thankfully, John Reed soon took over, and Citicorp became an enviable powerhouse. And The Executive was jettisoned to a premature retirement.

I tell this story because many of the biggest brands in America were once run by people like that. Complacency used to be rampant in the business world. Part of the explanation was probably generational.

Of course, there probably isn't a Baby Boomer or Gen-Xer in America who hasn't felt a little soft in comparison to the World War II generation he or she is now taking over for. After all, those people survived the Great Depression, kept the world safe for democracy, and went on to prosper in almost everything they did. Tom Brokaw's recent bestseller, *The Greatest Generation*, makes the case for them about as directly as it can be made: "This is the greatest generation any society has ever produced," he writes. He's largely right, of course. The self-confidence of the World War II generation was earned—it came out of bitter experience.

One small problem, however: This older generation of executives retired believing that they had not just seen the rough-and-tumble of war, but also had seen the rough-and-tumble of *business*. And on that small point, I beg to differ. By today's standards, these heroes of the three-martini lunch were playing a country club game.

Twenty or 30 years ago, if you had a good solid brand, it tended to stay good and solid for a long time. Big players ruled: CBS, NBC, and ABC controlled television; Sears dominated retailing to the middle class. AT&T owned telecom, and the U.S. Post Office owned the mail delivery business. The life insurance business might have been a little more fragmented, but we were all reasonably happy. We knew who the competition was, we were making plenty of money, and no one threatened our business model.

In fact, the big life insurance players all did business the same way: We pushed our products through agents who went door to door and earned big upfront commissions on every policy they sold. For consumers, it was the most expensive, time-consuming, and intrusive of all possible ways of delivering life insurance, but that didn't matter: The Prus, the Mets, and the John Hancocks were *the* only places they could buy this stuff.

Then, when the Fidelitys and the Schwabs started appearing and siphoning off dollars into their mutual funds that would once have gone to life insurance, and when new players started selling life insurance through new distribution channels at a lower cost than we could, the guys at the top of the industry sat around saying, "Who's going to buy mutual funds when they could buy life insurance?" And later, they said, "Who's going to buy life insurance from these newly branded companies when they could buy it from us?"

Clearly, the life insurance industry at least was waiting for a fall, but for decades it didn't happen. It used to be very difficult for upstarts in many industries to catch any traction, mainly because there was only one way to establish a new brand: Advertise on network television. This actively discouraged new players from entering the arena. Network TV was prohibitively expensive. Plus, it was insanely wasteful: The demographic group you were targeting might represent only 10 or 20 percent of the network audience. The rest of the impressions you paid so much for would be throwaways. And network TV actually deterred innovation: Because you were paying for a mass audience, you'd be forced to make your products more generic to appeal to as wide a group as possible.

It cost such a huge amount of money to launch a brand that the marketplace was dominated by major corporations. They were like sumo wrestlers pushing each other around on mats. Their only competition was each other. And naturally, the conventional wisdom about branding reflected this inertia. The idea was that brands had to be built over a long period of time, and the more established you were in people's minds, the better. One theory called "double jeopardy" suggested that brands with large market share not only were bought by more consumers, but also were bought more *often* by more *loyal* consumers. In other words, all the advantages were thought to go to the incumbents. Some people even thought market share was static. The number-one brand simply stayed the number-one brand, no matter what.

So why wouldn't you be arrogant if you were IBM or Sears or the U.S. Post Office? And why wouldn't you dismiss any other way of doing business except the one that kept you on top? After all, who's going to want a personal computer? Why would anyone need to buy any other brand of appliance but Kenmore? And what's the big deal with overnight delivery, anyway?

It's amusing to consider the idea that all the advantages go to the established brands in light of today's marketplace.

Brands that once seemed invincible—JCPenney, Sears, AT&T, the U.S. Post Office, and the "Big Three" television networks— are now just shadows of their former selves. Newer names have taken their place in the consciousness of the American consumer: The Gap, Home Depot, Sprint, FedEx, CNBC, and the WB Network. The landscape of business now looks like a series of earthquakes, as the Mount Everests crumble and upstarts who truly understand consumers rise out of nowhere to take their place. Every week, another big American brand wakes up out of a deep Rip Van Winkle sleep and finds that upstarts are shaking the ground out from under it. And the pace of change is only accelerating: Companies like eBay and Amazon.com that did not even exist a few years ago are now dominant brands in their fields.

We're not watching sumo wrestling anymore. Instead, the marketplace looks more like the bazaar scene in *Raiders of the Lost Ark*, where there's a big, menacing guy dressed in black, swinging a saber. He thinks he's tough until Harrison Ford pulls out a gun and shoots him. It's no longer the biggest guy who wins, but the fastest, smartest guy with the best command of new technologies.

THE CONSUMER REVOLUTION

Three very important events toppled the "sumo" brands. First, consumers' attitudes changed. The Baby Boomers were better educated than their parents and constitutionally less accepting of the status quo. Everything from Vietnam to Watergate to the

Exxon Valdez disaster taught them that big institutions were not to be trusted. And suspicion of big corporations has proved to have real endurance as a pop-culture concept. In just the last few years, the movie *A Civil Action* had John Travolta battling Beatrice and W. R. Grace; *The Insider* had Russell Crowe and Al Pacino fighting Brown & Williamson; and *Erin Brockovich* had Julia Roberts shooting down PG&E.

Guess who came out looking better: Julia Roberts, overflowing her miniskirt and bustier, or the big utility brand, leaking poison from its wastewater ponds? It is a small step in this world from rich corporation to villain, and any big brand that doesn't keep that constantly in mind is foolish.

The second thing that's happened is that thanks to technology and the explosion of media outlets, it now costs a fraction of what it once did to enter a business and create a brand. The "high-tech company born in a garage" myth has been around for some time now, but the Internet has lifted the ability of intelligent people to launch a business on a shoestring to another level entirely. Jeff Bezos got Amazon.com off the ground with $300,000 of his parents' retirement savings. Pierre Omidyar launched eBay with no more resources than his own ability to write code and a $30-a-month Internet service. Yahoo! was launched in a trailer by two procrastinating Ph.D. candidates who were more interested in creating an Internet index than in doing the work they were supposed to be doing.

Whatever struggles upstart companies eventually face down the road, technology has made it easier than ever for them to at least get onto the field.

And whether you're in a new-world business or old, it's no longer only those corporations that can afford to advertise on the network evening news that speak to consumers. Two-thirds of American households now have cable television, which means that today there are 40, 50, or 60 channels you can use to reach them. There were also almost 18,000 consumer magazines in 1999, according to *The National Directory of Magazines*—a 40-percent increase over the number just 10 years earlier.

With its several billion pages, the Web offers a nearly infinite variety of ways to reach consumers. And e-mail has turned word of mouth into a force to be reckoned with. Within its first 30 days in business, without any press or advertising, Amazon.com was able to sell books in all 50 states and 45 countries. Jeff Bezos simply asked 300 of his friends and family members to spread the word. When it comes to the Internet, six degrees of separation is probably five too many.

The demographic cuts are so fine in these new media outlets that you can speak to precisely the right audience. For a fraction of the money you'd have spent on network television, you can run commercials on the Lifetime Channel, the Discovery Channel, or the Food Network and create a subcult for your brand. You can advertise in *Teen People, Brill's Content,* or *Fine Gardening* and use the Internet on the backswing. Suddenly, you've grabbed market share from the established brand that seemed to be king. And there's a good chance that the established company did not even see you coming.

The result, in almost any product category you can name, from microbrewed beer to mutual funds, is an exploding number of brand choices for consumers.

The third leg of this revolution is the unlimited access to information that consumers now have. What's occurred is the business equivalent of the fall of the Soviet Union. The Marxist state survived as long as it did only because it controlled the flow of information. It was the "mushroom" theory of public relations: "Feed 'em horse manure and keep 'em in the dark."

The Marxist capitalists—the big dominant corporations of the past—maintained their power in a similar fashion. Consumers had only limited access to information and distributors; therefore, corporations had to give them only limited choices. The pre-Internet marketplace was not unlike a Moscow grocery store before the fall of Communism: You could have the brown sausage, or you could have the white sausage, but you were *going* to have sausage.

Thanks to the Internet, however, consumers are no longer limited to what their local retailers are willing to stock, and comparison shopping no longer means expending considerable shoe leather interviewing a number of dubiously trustworthy salespeople. No matter what the consumer is searching for, from bird cages to mutual funds, a half-hour online will generate enough information to turn him or her into a walking, talking *Consumer Reports*.

The old economy was a product-push economy. Manufacturers made what they wanted to make, at the cost structures they liked. And then salespeople pushed those products off onto a gullible public. The new economy is a marketing economy, with the consumer firmly in charge.

WHEN THE CONSUMER RULES, ARROGANCE KILLS

Charles de Gaulle put his finger on the political implications of consumer choice when he expressed his own exasperation with the French: "How can you govern a country that has 246 kinds of cheese?" The truth is consumers who have that many choices are ungovernable, especially by despots. Choice teaches consumers to make increasingly fine distinctions between what they like and what they don't. In the process, it raises the bar for anyone trying to sell them anything from a political idea to shampoo.

Not surprisingly, many of the brands that ruled in a world in which consumers had less power are also-rans today. The truth is, brands are much more vulnerable than the executives in the dominant corporations of the past ever believed them to be. It was a particular collection of historical circumstances that kept many brands on top for so long, but the top executives of these brands mistook the size of their market share for the genius of their management. And now many of those brands are fighting for their very identity.

It's a pattern repeated over and over: Big companies that mismanage once-strong brands suddenly find themselves slipping in consumers' eyes. They go through a period of bad publicity and falling sales, and falling sales and bad publicity, that feels almost like a death spiral. Of course, many of them recover, mainly because their huge reserves of capital keep them from crashing completely. The best of them, like IBM, remake themselves into modern competitors, but none of them ever seem to achieve the same dominant market share they once had. They may be among the top brands, but the top is now shared.

Clearly, the arrogant old dinosaurs offer plenty of lessons in how not to win friends and influence people. But that leaves another question open: How *do* you compete in a world in which consumers have infinite knowledge and choice?

You can trade in commodities and try to win on price alone, a depressing downward spiral, given the almost limitless competition most businesses face today. That's why, in many industries, the smart commodities producers are turning their commodities into brands and commanding a premium for them. Increasingly, consumers no longer just reach for milk; they reach for Horizon Organic milk at almost twice the price. They don't drink unbranded water from the well or from the reservoir; they drink Evian or one of hundreds of other brands of bottled water at over a dollar for a little bottle.

If you don't want to compete on price alone, you can, of course, try to win on product features or service. But technology makes it unlikely that you'll offer anything that can't be copied by your competitors in record time.

Or you can join the battle of the brands. In that case, everything you once thought was important—margins, service, information systems, and even the products you sell—will have to become subservient to the brand. Because no matter how well you do these other things, consumers will never notice if there isn't an appealing brand out in front whistling for their attention.

Business theorists are now talking about the emergence of the "experience" or "entertainment" economy, in which the most successful companies no longer sell goods or services, but instead sell an experience. This is just what Nike, for example, does in its spectacular NikeTown stores. It's not selling athletic shoes based on product features; it's getting the consumer to buy those shoes by enshrining the whole idea of athletic competition. Starbucks is another example. No one would ever accuse it of just selling coffee. Instead, it sells the entire coffeehouse experience, meticulously controlled down to the reading material offered at the counter, which even included, for a time, its own magazine, *Joe*.

Actually, the phenomenon is at once simpler and broader than the ascendancy of shopping as entertainment, and it applies to brands like John Hancock that will never offer a purchasing experience that can be confused with a trip to Disneyland. It is simply human nature for people to prefer the richer experience to the more austere. And the experience of purchasing anything is richer if you buy a good brand, since a whole host of pleasant associations, by definition, accompanies that brand.

Why is it the brand, stupid? Because consumers have so many choices today, there is no reason for them to buy anything that doesn't give them enjoyment. Strong brands are simply more enjoyable to buy, so you'd better have one if you hope to compete.

2

CODEPENDENCY CAN BE BEAUTIFUL

CONSUMERS NEED GOOD BRANDS AS MUCH AS GOOD BRANDS NEED THEM

John Hancock's hometown of Boston is a funny place. It's probably one of the few cities in the world today where the ruling powers prefer wearing Brooks Brothers to Armani and view Armani as slightly déclassé, because if you put on an Armani suit, you won't look like a butcher block. Instead, you'll look as if you actually intend to look good.

The thing that sets Boston apart from many of America's other less glossy locales is that it is not a benighted old industrial city where people simply do not have the money or the exposure

15

to care about style. Instead, it is a rich, sophisticated city with a thriving cultural life that is nonetheless highly suspicious of material display. It's easy to trace the influences here: the Brahmins, with their Puritan abhorrence of any form of vulgar show; the Cambridge academics, who would like to believe they have their minds on higher things; and the new high-tech elite, who consider the more casual the better. Add these groups together, and you create a place where it is not fashionable to be fashionable.

As a result, if you travel anywhere in Boston, you tend to hear people say, "I never think about brands. I just buy what's there," or "I have no idea who made it. It's just something I picked up in Filene's Basement years ago."

I have noticed one thing, however: Even in academic Cambridge, among the crunchies, it's not a *real* sandal unless it's a Birkenstock.

A lot of people think they don't pay attention to brands. But usually, they do—they may just pay attention to the opposition brands, the rebel brands, or the cult brands. They allow their distaste for the dominant brands to convince them they are too high-minded to hear the siren song of the marketers.

When I meet them, I like to give these "brand-immune" types a small test. I ask them to imagine that they need to buy a list of things—a washing machine, a car, and maybe even underwear. Then I ask them what they would buy and how they'd choose it. Almost infallibly, I hear a big brand name, followed by the statement of belief that the brand makes a good product. I have almost never heard anyone say they'd make their choices by conducting their own examinations with a screwdriver, a wrench, and an itch test.

The truth is that no matter what is in question—where to send the children to school or what kind of potato chip to buy—no one is capable of pulling out the screwdriver and wrench every time and considering every case on its merits. Life is too complicated for that. So we're conditioned to respond to brands of all kinds. They help us organize our experience and tell us what to pursue and what to reject. And we use these brands not just to make purchasing decisions, but also to make life decisions. For example, I actually dated a woman once who said she couldn't continue seeing me because my name is David and she'd had bad experiences with Davids. For her, David was no longer a desirable brand.

Clearly, this woman was a tad literal-minded, but the impulse is one we all share. We'd never survive without archetypes, predispositions, and antipathies to give us at least a starting point for comprehending any given situation. Brands are simply the manufactured equivalent of the shorthand we use to interpret the world in general.

Is the woman we're being introduced to a blonde, a redhead, or a brunette? We make certain assumptions about her personality instinctively, depending on which hair color commands the foreground. Of course, these assumptions may be dead wrong, but they at least give us a way to begin figuring out who she is. Is the dress Prada or Versace? Again, we have different assumptions of one brand over the other—and of the woman who wears one over the other.

Ultimately, brands are a kind of language for American consumers. And most of us understand that a simple statement like "I stopped at Starbucks on the way to the office" contains another, more subtle, brand-based meaning as well: "I really do have a bit of bohemian in me despite the corporate job." This brand-based language is by no means a primitive language, either. I am constantly astonished at people's capacity for keeping a vast number of brands in their head at once.

Of course, the words in this language are constantly changing and, in fact, they *have* to change. In order to define itself, each generation feels compelled to "dis" the previous generation's brands. A *Boston Magazine* sidebar to a story titled "X Marks Its Spot" pinpoints the differences between Generation X and the Baby Boomers with a list that includes a number of opposing brands: British Airways for the Boomers, Virgin Atlantic for the Xers; FleetBank for the Boomers, Wingspan Bank for the Xers; the *Boston Globe* for the Boomers, Salon.com for the Xers. What hasn't changed between the generations, however, is their attachment to certain brands. If anything, over time, consumers seem to be growing more attached to brands, not less.

Ultimately, people not only *prefer* good brands to weak ones, they actually *need* them, and they may need them more than ever. The incredible plethora of choices consumers now possess has a downside, and it's called exhaustion. An overwhelming number of possibilities complicates every buying decision. Add to that all the other more baroque aspects of modern life, such as two-income households, frequent divorce and remarriage and blending of families, increasing traffic, shortening news cycles, and 100 channels of cable television, and you wind up with a consumer group that feels very overloaded and harassed.

It's a paradox: The more brands consumers have to choose from, the more they need to cling to one good brand.

Good brands do three highly significant things for stressed-out consumers:

1. They save time.
2. They project the right message.
3. They provide an identity.

SAVING TIME

First, good brands save time for the consumer, because there is no need to survey an entire product category. The best brand equals the best product. This equation is unshakable, even when it flies in the face of logic. Even consumers who know—who absolutely *know*—that two products are exactly the same tend to choose the one with the bigger brand name.

Over-the-counter drugs are a great example. If your baby has a fever, you're far more likely to buy Tylenol over the generic acetaminophen. The active ingredients are the same, and the generic might save you a third of the price; nonetheless, chances are that you will choose the brand name. In fact, Children's Tylenol actually outsells all its competitors combined. One study showed that Tylenol users are particularly "bonded" to the brand. It's not rational, but most consumers just feel better about Tylenol.

Of course, no one would pay a third more for an identical piece of window glass just because it has a brand name. But, then, less is at stake with window glass. The closer the product gets to the consumer physically, the more the brand matters. *If they wear—or particularly if they ingest—it, they want the comfort of a brand name.*

PROJECTING THE RIGHT MESSAGE

The second thing good brands do is project the right message to the people who'll be judging you. They're headache-avoidance devices. When you're making cheesecake for your hypercritical mother, it's a good bet that you'll choose the Philadelphia Cream Cheese over the supermarket brand because you know how the Philadelphia brand tastes, and you don't want any problems. The equivalent mindset operates in business, under the old data-processing managers' motto, "No one ever got fired for buying IBM." Even if there is trouble down the road, no one can fault you for choosing the brand with the sturdiest reputation.

This is why, when John Hancock converted from a mutual insurer to a publicly traded stock company early in 2000, we chose Morgan Stanley as the lead underwriter for our initial public offering (IPO). We told ourselves that we liked the people there, but that was not the real reason Morgan Stanley got our business. Most investment bankers look alike, like hypergroomed guys who flunked out of weather forecasting school. All of them are smart, and there were many other investment banks that would have loved to have gotten the deal. But we picked Morgan Stanley because it had the best reputation. Even if the IPO failed, no one would criticize us for choosing Morgan Stanley.

And the fact that the IPO was a success has to be credited partly to the underwriter's reputation. It got us in the door with investors who might not otherwise have considered buying our stock.

PROVIDING AN IDENTITY

The third thing good brands do is give people an identity that makes them feel secure, as if they belong to a group of like-minded travelers. In his brilliant intellectual history *The Americans: The Democratic Experience*, Daniel J. Boorstin characterizes these "consumption communities" created by brands as a particularly American phenomenon. He describes their appearance at the end of the 19th and the beginning of the 20th century this way:

> The advertisers of nationally branded products constantly told their constituents that by buying their products they could join a special group, and millions of Americans were eager to join. . . . Their members recognized one another, sharing certain illusions, hopes, and disappointments . . . .
> The modern American then, was tied, if only by the thinnest of threads and by the most volatile, switchable loyalties, to thousands of other Americans in nearly everything he ate or drank or drove or read or used.[1]

Boorstin points out that these communities created by brand loyalties were not as intensely meaningful as those communities

[1] Daniel J. Boorstin, *The Americans: The Democratic Experience* (New York: Vintage Books, 1974) pp. 147–48.

21

that arose earlier in American history out of shared religious and political ideologies. Nonetheless, they were the product of a country that at the turn of the last century had two groups of people who needed above all to belong: a widely dispersed, lonely rural population and a tremendous number of new immigrants. National brands helped both groups to feel a part of the American culture at large.

Since the beginning of the 20th century, of course, improvements in technology, transportation, and the social fabric of the country have made the connections we forge ever more mobile, wide ranging, and ad hoc. And the tribes we belong to are determined even less by geography, pedigree, race, or religion. Instead, our tribes are determined largely by education and accomplishment, and they are manifested by the things we consume.

More and more, they are *brand* tribes. And if you don't believe you're subject to such affiliations, ask yourself this: With whom are you more likely to share what Boorstin calls "certain illusions, hopes, and disappointments"? With someone 3,000 miles away, who drinks the same brand of microbrewed beer as you do, or with the "Bud" drinker who lives right next door?

It's a strange truth—but a truth nonetheless—that we probably have far more in common with the person who drinks the same brand of beer as we do, but lives on the other side of the country, than we do with the person who happens merely to live on the same street, but has entirely different taste in a brew.

Of course, these brand tribes may be far subtler than they used to be. Back in the 1970s, you had to have a Calvin Klein label roughly the size of a Volkswagen on your rear end so people knew you were wearing Calvin Klein. Now, we have entire cities like New York and Los Angeles where people wear nothing but black. But most people can still tell in an instant whether the guy sitting across from them is wearing Gucci black or Prada black or Fruit of the Loom black. And it matters.

The smartest brands take advantage of this mindset by both going after and helping to define a tribe. Ann Taylor, for example, has zeroed in demographically on a certain kind of urban working woman in all age groups. If you go into an Ann Taylor store, 9 out of 10 women shopping there will already be dressed alike. Through a reliable combination of fit, styling, and brand message, the company has turned them all into Ann Taylor people.

Being an Ann Taylor person is profoundly comforting. You know how the jacket is going to fit before you put it on. You know the clothes are not going to be wild, nor are they going to be dowdy. You know they won't be too expensive or too cheaply made either. You'll come out of there looking stylish, but not trendy. As Goldilocks said about the baby bear's bed, "It's just right."

Brands as smart as this turn into cults. The consumer starts to feel uncomfortable in any other brand. He or she becomes addicted to the experience of buying your products. Entire households commit themselves to the brand. The family understands that if they buy Aunt Tracy an Ann Taylor outfit for Christmas, they are safe. It's her brand, and it gets them off the hook.

The exchange consumers make with a good brand like this makes perfect sense: The brand offers comfort, trust, convenience, and identity in an excessively complicated world. In return, consumers give the brand their predisposition to buy it over any other brand. This is a very pleasant state of codependency that every brand builder should work to achieve.

Of course, it would be a mistake to omit one final, crucial way that you can use your brand to simplify consumers' lives and give them some much-needed peace of mind. And that is by convincing them never, *ever* to buy your products again.

In the past, consumers might not have been able to afford to nurse a brand resentment; after all, the toy store that offended them might have been the only toy store within miles. Now, any brand that offends them can be immediately replaced by one of a dozen other brands, online or offline. And finding an excuse *not* to buy a brand can be just as enjoyable as finding an excuse to buy one. That, too, is human nature.

Let me tell you the story of my relationship with a certain national chain. In my part of the world, this chain has bought up a lot of little breakfast shops and eliminated the competition, which I don't particularly mind. Capitalism at work. And, after all, they're cleaner than their mom-and-pop predecessors. But here's what I do mind: Most of their stores have individual owners, and the quality of coffee, in my opinion, is inconsistent from one location to another. At one place, the coffee's too thin, at another too acidic, at still another it's been sitting around until it's turned to tar.

At one particular shop, the coffee was so terrible that I contacted a company official about it. I was being helpful. But in his reply, this official didn't say, "We're going to look into it." Instead, he insulted my intelligence by insisting that the quality of the coffee changes from one shop to another because of local water conditions.

Local water conditions had nothing to do with it, of course. It was obvious to me that the franchise owner was just watering down his coffee to take in another two cents a cup.

Needless to say, I no longer buy coffee at this shop, nor at any other shop in this chain, anywhere in the universe. Crossing this brand off my list has opened up all kinds of psychic space for me as a consumer; though I admit, it sometimes makes it hard to find a cup of coffee in the morning.

The truth is that consumers need brands, both good and bad, to help them navigate a world in which their choices are almost infinite. The best thing that can happen to a brand is to become a kind of shorthand in consumers' eyes for trustworthiness, style, excitement, or any of a host of other great qualities that demand their loyalty and respect.

Establishing the right brand message is the first step on that road. The next chapter will talk about how.

A GREAT BRAND MESSAGE IS LIKE A BUCKING BRONCO—ONCE YOU'RE ON, DON'T LET GO

The most important task of any brand builder is the brand message: figuring out what it ought to be if the brand is new, and understanding what it is and where it ought to go if the brand is already established.

The debate about which is easier—starting from scratch and creating a message for a new brand or remaking an existing brand—is eternal. The best public relations minds of William the Conqueror's court probably sat around over tankards of mead debating this very question. Was it easier to establish a new king in the hearts and minds of the people or to reposition an old king who had conquered their land and slain half the villagers and would now like to pass himself off as a benevolent leader?

Being the new king does have one great advantage over being an old one: At least you know where you are with the people—you're nowhere.

ESTABLISHING A NEW BRAND IN THE INTERNET AGE

Anyone hoping to glean some insight into the dos and don'ts of establishing a new brand could hardly do better than to study the feeding frenzy among the second wave of Internet startups, the ones that suddenly became major advertisers in 1999 and 2000. What makes these companies such fascinating case studies is that they had the exact opposite of what most new brands have: They had real money to spend, thanks to that brief moment when every tech-stock IPO was a rocket ride to the stratosphere and venture capital was easier to obtain than a driver's license.

Of course, the first wave of e-commerce players such as Amazon.com and eBay didn't need vast advertising budgets to establish their brands: They were able to send their brands out into the world through word of mouth and the Internet itself. Inevitably, however, the novelty that would convince the average web-head to e-mail the address of some new e-commerce site to his or her 500 closest friends began to wear off. So the second-wave Internet brands were forced to turn to the old media to get their message out.

And, turn to it they did, with a vengeance, spending billions on advertising by 1999. The dot-coms dominated the 2000 Super Bowl and other televised sporting events and took over the glossy magazines.

What did they get for all that money? Gerbils exploding out of cannons, *Star Trek* star William Shatner parodying his own brief singing career of 30 years ago, people walking down a city street quoting Robert Frost, and a madeup saint called Lucy of Portland. At the end of the commercial or print ad, you generally still didn't know who they were or what they did or why you should bother. But the advertisement was kind of interesting nonetheless, so you were grateful for the entertainment.

As brand builders, the dot-coms of the late 1990s were fascinated with their own obliqueness. They were trying to out-subtle each other. The brand message was: "We're too new world to be direct."

It's easy to imagine the thinking behind all this intentional obscurity. First of all, even though these brands could no longer rely solely on the underground network to establish themselves, as Amazon.com once did, they were probably anxious to keep the spirit of the underground alive in their brand-building efforts, since it worked so well for their predecessors.

Second, I suspect many of them were influenced by the greatest high-tech commercial of all time and one of the greatest product introductions ever: Apple's 1984 Super Bowl commercial for the new Macintosh computer. The spot takes off from George Orwell's *1984*, with a room full of slaves being lectured to by Big Brother on a giant screen until they're liberated by a beautiful, athletic woman in an Apple T-shirt, who throws a sledgehammer at the screen. The product itself was never seen in this particular spot. It was a pure brand message, and the message was outrageous and grandiose. Apple was basically calling itself the savior of mankind. The spot was exceptional in other ways as well. It was visually stunning. Ridley Scott, who's made a number of striking movies, including *Blade Runner* and *Gladiator*, directed it. But the most incredible thing about the spot was the fact that Apple only paid to run it once, yet no one who saw it has ever forgotten it. An excellent model that no startup brand should even *consider* trying to imitate, as I'll explain in a moment.

I suspect the third reason so many Internet branding campaigns have been so obscure is that many of these companies are run by engineers, not marketers. Engineers, by definition, are adept at the kind of communications that involve electrical signals, not the kind that involve seduction and persuasion.

The fourth reason for these puzzling campaigns is the perpetual spinelessness of advertising agencies, most of which will feed their clients *anything* they want so long as they can pay for it.

And the fifth reason is that there *was* a certain legitimacy to the Esperanto these new brands were speaking. There is no question that the dot-coms have taught the world to speak their language, rather than the other way around. When dignified Boston law firms like Hale and Dorr and Goodwin Procter adopt "casual dress" policies in order to better relate to their high-tech clients, it's clear that even the proudest old business cultures have given way to the culture of Silicon Valley.

It's one thing, however, to force your *lawyer* to change his or her stripes to please you. In asking *consumers* to meet them more than halfway, many of the new Internet brands made a few classic mistakes.

ONLY ESTABLISHED BRANDS ARE ALLOWED TO BE OBSCURE

Apple's *1984* ad worked because consumers already knew what Apple was and what it did. You cannot afford to be that oblique unless people know who you are to begin with. That's one of the great advantages of established brands. John Hancock is able to get away with cinema verité commercials—little slices of life that don't seem like commercials until the company's logo appears quietly at the end—because our brand is firmly established in people's minds. What John Hancock does is not the issue. Nike has done brilliant brand-building commercials that most viewers can't even recognize as commercials until the "Just Do It" tagline appears in the last second, or they see the flash of a swoosh on someone's clothing. These spots work because Nike is already such a powerful presence in consumers' minds, that its failure to say "We sell running shoes" only makes the shoes that much more alluring.

When the typical e-commerce startup, on the other hand, attempted to be similarly oblique, the result was a complete disconnect. Since you didn't know who it was or what it did, you had no idea what it was talking about.

Here's a prime example: online computer and electronics retailer Cyberian Outpost's outrageous first television campaign. It included a commercial that showed gerbils being shot out of a cannon toward a wall painted with the word "Outpost." The spot was both shocking and funny. The company spent big to run it during the 1999 Super Bowl. It garnered an enormous amount of media attention. But from the brand standpoint, it was a failure. The commercial might have gotten consumers to remember the Outpost name, but it gave them very little idea what the company did. Fortunately, Outpost.com soon hired an experienced CEO who made sure the company sent two messages to consumers: that it offered free overnight shipping and that it sold "technology, not gerbils."

A new brand had better spend some time on the prosaic stuff, such as what the company does and why the consumer should bother.

IT'S NOT THE IDEA THAT RULES, IT'S THE EXECUTION

The brand-building campaigns of many e-commerce companies have celebrated inventiveness and outrageousness for their own sake. This emphasis on originality at the expense of everything else is a natural temptation for companies that are still driven by the entrepreneurs who had the original idea that begat the company.

Unfortunately, in most human endeavors, it is seldom the idea itself that winds up being the most valuable thing. The pattern has been the same since Neanderthal times. In the cave, the genius who invented the club was rewarded only temporarily; the pragmatic types who went out and used the club to kill game every day were the ones who were rewarded over the long haul. And the inventor probably spent the next 20 years grumbling about not getting enough credit for it.

For every new startup that succeeds, a hundred will fail because they cannot launch their brands. And the winners will not be the most gifted engineers and the most dashing entrepreneurs, but the best marketers.

Real marketers know that brand building is not about celebrating your own iconoclastic spirit. It's about communicating with consumers, and that means that someone on the other side of the television, radio, or newspaper has to *understand*.

Of course, it's not just Internet startups that find themselves staring at their own navels when they should instead be trying to communicate. In the 1970s, when I was working for the computer company Control Data, the division I worked for had no presence in Japan and wanted one. So we took our division's name, had it translated into Japanese in New York, and copied the symbols onto everything, expecting to soon take the Japanese market by storm.

There was just one obstacle: We had to get the permission of half a dozen Japanese ministries to do business there. So we dutifully ran around to all the appropriate bureaucrats, and we spent many hours, many months, and many millions of dollars sitting in conference rooms with them. They would bow and smile, yet we could never finally get their okay to proceed.

It turns out, what the ministers were too polite to tell us was that our name in Japanese, loosely translated, meant "We Give Gonorrhea." I'm not sure whether the translator we had used for the logo was vengeful or incompetent, but the point is, we never checked his work with our intended market. The ministers thought we were just stupid, and they were not far off the mark.

A BRAND MESSAGE HAS TO SPEAK TO CONSUMERS

There are, however, some e-commerce companies that have done a very good job of introducing themselves to their intended markets. The online securities broker E*Trade, for example, has been particularly effective at establishing its brand. Of course, like most online merchants, E*Trade is easy to use, convenient, and reasonably priced. But in its advertising, the company does not focus on product features or price. Instead, it focuses on the extra-added attraction offered by the brand: Use E*Trade and you get to screw the old economy.

The company website was launched in 1996 with print ads that announced, "Your broker is now obsolete," and it has mercilessly attacked the old full-service stockbroker ever since. A 1999 commercial featured the tag line, "If your broker's so great, how come he still has to work?"

Other E*Trade commercials have jabbed at the full range of humiliations people have endured hoping to become rich, including asking the boss for a raise, catering to an elderly "sugar mama," watching personal empowerment infomercials, playing the lottery, and listening to the bozos who call in to talk shows on cable television. The tone of these ads reminds me of the movie *Network,* with Peter Finch inciting people to shout, "I'm mad as hell, and I'm not going to take it anymore." A mild-mannered way to distinguish yourself from the rest of the securities industry, this is not. Christos Cotsakos, E*Trade's CEO, has admitted as much: "We are zealots," he said, "and this is a jihad."

However, E*Trade differs from a lot of other edgy e-commerce brands in that it is not bragging about its *own* rebelliousness. Instead, it is selling itself as an opportunity for *consumers* to rebel against the old economy. Its brand message offers something of essential value to consumers: sweet revenge against every financial advisor who has ever done them wrong.

And that message goes a long way toward explaining why this particular upstart managed to pull ahead of even a strong investment brand like Fidelity in the online brokerage market and quickly reach a dynamic number-two spot, right behind Charles Schwab.

A STRONG BRAND MESSAGE REQUIRES TWO KINDS OF KNOWLEDGE AND ONE KIND OF DISCIPLINE

The truth is that the best brands, like the most interesting people, have a keen sense of self. Self-knowledge can save you from a world of mistakes. For example, Mickey Drexler, the man who's made the Gap the most powerful mass-market clothing brand in America, was horrified by a set of new print ads in 1996 that linked the Gap to heroin chic. The strung-out look might have been fashionable at the time, but as Drexler told *Fortune* magazine, "It was so incompatible in my mind with what made Gap right." He quickly put an end to that campaign.

At the very best companies, every employee within the organization shares this same instinctive grasp of the brand message.

However, as important as it is to know *who* you are in order to establish a strong brand message, it's also equally important to know *where* you are. In other words, you have to understand what your brand means not within the confines of your offices, but out in the world, where the consumers are.

The problem with consumer research, of course, is that you can spend tens of millions of dollars on surveys designed to do nothing but confirm your inner thoughts. Although everyone says they do it, very few businesses are actually any good at listening to consumers. Most people in power are not interested in the truth, but this is an executive's primary job, the search for the truth.

If you want your brand to succeed, you'd better have an honest grasp of at least a few fundamentals: How aware are people of your brand? What is your brand known for? Is it about trust? Price? Diligence? Thoroughness? What *is* it about? What do people *not* like about your brand? In fact, what do people not like about your industry? What about the people who distribute your brand? How do consumers feel about them?

Done right, this kind of research will give you a starting point for all your communications and a baseline to measure against over time. Without it, you may as well be playing pin the tail on the donkey with your marketing efforts.

A conglomerate called Beatrice offers a classic example of what a lack of self-awareness can do to a brand. By the mid-1980s, Beatrice had swallowed up a lot of packaged goods companies and wound up with dozens of strong brands to its credit, such as Peter Pan peanut butter, Hunts ketchup, Samsonite luggage, Butterball turkeys, and Stiffel lamps.

Then someone at the home office decided that these individual brands were not as important as the relatively unknown corporate brand. So the company ran an overwhelming television campaign that no one understood, showing a ketchup bottle, a suitcase, and a turkey, announcing, "We're Beatrice." All on the theory, I suppose, that consumers would say, "I'm going to buy that ketchup because Beatrice makes it. God, Almighty, what was I thinking! Why would I buy any other ketchup?" Or perhaps an even more convoluted marketing strategy was in play. Maybe the idea was that consumers would say, "Beatrice makes a great ketchup. It must make great lamps!"

The truth is, the Beatrice brand was meaningless to consumers. In the packaged goods business, the master brand is almost never as important as the individual brands underneath it. Gillette, for example, owns Oral B, but the company is too smart to broadcast that to consumers. It knows very well that consumers do not want to buy a toothbrush made by a razor-blade company.

Millions and millions of dollars were spent blowing Beatrice's horn, and absolutely nothing of any importance whatsoever was communicated to consumers. Well, here is a surefire way to wish yourself out of existence: use your marketing dollars to pump yourself up instead of talking to consumers about the things that matter to them. I don't think it's any coincidence that Beatrice is now defunct.

After self-knowledge and self-awareness, the final thing required for a strong brand message is discipline. When you think about it, the job of the brand builder is not very different from that of the political operative. And here's what sets the good political campaign manager apart: He or she figures out a message that, first, suits the product the voters are asked to buy; and that, second, speaks to the voters. Then he or she drives that message home like a spear, until the product is identified with nothing else and the voters cannot resist this juggernaut.

Lee Atwater, former President George Bush's chief strategist during the 1988 presidential race, basically determined that the campaign hinged on its ability to paint Mike Dukakis as an out-of-touch liberal. The campaign was so disciplined about this that Atwater predicted that Willie Horton would wind up as Dukakis's running mate. (Willie Horton was the convicted murderer given furloughs from prison under the Dukakis administration in Massachusetts. He became the Republican's poster child for Dukakis's stance on crime.) When Bush won in 1988, Atwater was hailed as a genius, albeit a diabolical genius. However, by 1992, Atwater had died an untimely death, and James Carville was able to use an equal focus on the right message for the moment—"The economy, stupid"—to defeat Bush and put Clinton in the White House.

Brand builders need a similar form of discipline. At John Hancock, we determined years ago that we wanted to set ourselves apart from the rest of the country's insurance companies, all those cold organizations that had enshrined themselves in their mausoleum-like real estate, with brand messages which announced that they were as unfeeling as granite. In some ways, life insurance *is* a very cold business, like bookmaking and loan-sharking. We bet you'll live longer than you're willing to risk, and then we loan out—or invest—the money you give us at an attractive rate of return. But at John Hancock, we did not think we had much to gain by broadcasting the coolly calculating nature of our business to consumers.

Instead, we created a brand that is all about empathy. We don't brag about ourselves; we demonstrate that we understand the fears and hopes of our customers. And we're extremely focused about it. We simply do not make commercials that say, "You can buy any financial services product you want from us." If the commercial does not express our empathy with the consumer, we don't make it. If the sports sponsorship cannot be used to tell our potential customers that we share their concerns, we don't buy into it.

KEEPING THE MESSAGE RELEVANT

The one significant difference between running a political campaign and building a brand is that in the case of the brand, the campaign never ends. As difficult as it is to find the right message in the first place, it's even more difficult to hang onto it. And that is because brands cannot simply stand still. They must pull off the neat trick of retaining all the goodwill they've built up throughout history while changing with the times—and they have to pull off this trick again and again.

No company provides a better object lesson in the importance of staying relevant than Levi Strauss & Co. One of America's great brands, Levi's lost more than half its share of the American jeans market during the 1990s, and its sales fell 28 percent between 1996 and 1999 alone. The company simply failed to invest in Gen-X and the Echo Boom. For a long time, Levi's seemed not to understand that kids no longer wore the tight-legged jeans it was producing. It failed to perceive that hip young people no longer shopped in the tired old department stores that were its main distributors. Instead of saying to the young, "You should come to us because we'll make you look cool," Levi's brand message was an arrogant "You should come to us because we're the inventor of jeans."

Of course, Levi's branding has always been about the company's history and authenticity. Conveying a sense of history is fine, but getting calcified is not. And failing to offer anything of value to young people eager to distinguish themselves from the previous generation is lethal.

Levi's forgot one simple principle: Kids will go out of their way not to wear what their parents wore. Fresh out of college myself, I once had the unenviable assignment of researching the personal grooming habits of the young for Gillette. This was at the height of hippiedom, when teenagers washed their hair once a week, if that. I'll never forget one guy patiently explaining to me, "Look, you have to understand. I won't buy anything that my father buys. I won't buy Old Spice, I won't buy Gillette, I won't buy Aqua Velva. My *whole objective* is not to smell like my father." And I had to report back to Gillette that it was not going to break into this market.

Unfortunately, some brands grow so out of touch that there is almost nothing you can do to change public perception and make them seem contemporary. The retailer Montgomery Ward—aka "monkey ward"—comes to mind on this score. Incarnation after incarnation and store modernization after store modernization failed to alter its brand message: the dowdiest merchandise displayed in the most depressing way. Owner GE Capital finally pulled the plug on the 128-year-old brand in late 2000.

Although it's difficult to remake an old brand that says the wrong things in the marketplace, it's not impossible if you listen to consumers in the right ways. In the mid-1990s, Wolverine, the company that makes Hush Puppies, was stumped about how to resurrect a terminally unfashionable brand. Edgier advertising, for example, was not working. But then the company got reports that New York City kids were snapping up vintage Hush Puppies in thrift stores. And it was smart enough to use that intelligence to turn a little blip into a trend. By forging relationships with fashion designers who helped it update and exploit Hush Puppies' "retro-cool" look, Wolverine wound up with a huge hit on its hands.

The classic consumer research may tell you what the average consumer thinks, but it will never help you find the hot spots in the culture where the trends are being born that you can ride to exploding sales. Any brand hoping to update itself could do far worse than zero in on the little hot pockets of people who *are* buying it and try to learn why.

KEEPING THE MESSAGE CONSISTENT

For every brand that loses its way because it fails to keep its message fresh, another loses its way because it fails to keep its message consistent. Every brand builder will face a million temptations to obscure, dilute, or confuse his or her brand message. These temptations fall under two general headings: boredom and the desire for growth.

Let's talk about the first: boredom. The truth is, the people on the inside of a company spend a lot of time with the brand, and they get tired of it a lot more quickly than the consumer does. The classic situation involves a promotion. Suddenly, somebody new is VP of marketing or CEO of the entire company. That person has the new job and the corner office. He or she has already redecorated and hung new pictures on the wall. And now it's time to put his or her personal stamp on the brand. That person will predictably say, "We're taking the best of the old and adding the best of the new" and wind up with something thoroughly convoluted that drives consumers away. The only people who make money on this kind of executive preening are advertising agencies, graphic designers, and the people who print the company stationery.

For example, one senior executive of John Hancock actually insisted that we drop the famous John Hancock signature from our logo and replace it with personality-free block letters. Never mind that we'd been using the signature since 1862, and it was one of America's oldest logos and spoke volumes about our trustworthiness and stability. Never mind that we had a trademark recognized by anyone who'd ever sat through a fifth-grade history class, and by removing it, he almost cost us our right to use it. He was apparently tired of it. Fortunately, he soon left the company, along with his block letters.

Of course, the fatuousness of corporate executives is a minor danger to good brands, compared with the incessant pressure for growth every public company faces. Sooner or later, this pressure leads most companies to attempt to extend their brands to new products and even new businesses. And given the omnivorousness of today's best-capitalized companies, we may well be entering a new era of ITT-style diversified conglomerates in which Disney, for example, buys a hog farm one day and a life insurer the next.

While it may make perfect sense to extend your brand to a closely related product—Miller adds Miller Lite, E*Trade adds online banking—even a sensible stretch like this has its risks and should not be done thoughtlessly.

As a young public relations consultant, I actually helped launch one of the worst brand extensions of all time. The client was National Distillers, and in the early 1970s the company was very worried about a steep decline in whisky consumption. Drunk-driving laws were getting harsher, and hard drinking was becoming less socially acceptable. People didn't want to fall asleep at their desks in the afternoons anymore, and they couldn't afford to have alcohol on their breath. Increasingly, they were drinking vodka instead of bourbon and wine instead of cocktails, even before dinner, all of which was just heresy to the distillers. They were furious about the situation.

So National Distillers, like a number of its competitors, developed something called a "light" whisky, under the Old Crow brand. Instead of being aged in the new charred oak barrels that give bourbon its characteristic red color and rich taste, "light" whisky was aged in used or uncharred barrels for a lighter color and taste. The idea was "Looks like Chardonnay, tastes like whisky."

National Distillers was doing the opposite of spotting a trend—it was stubbornly insisting that one could be bucked. And it was sure that Crow Light would knock those other pale liquors off their pedestals. The company's public relations firm, on the other hand, suspected that the product was doomed to failure. In the focus group studies we did, people absolutely hated the stuff. One guy wanted to put it in his car's gas tank.

I was assigned to the account as the lead player, and I knew we had to do something outrageous to get some attention. We scheduled a press party at the Park Lane Hotel in New York, and I went to Long Island to meet a guy who trained animals for Hollywood movies, hoping we could get a crow for the party. Not only did he have a crow, he had a crow so well trained, it would relieve itself whenever he blew a little whistle.

He also had carrier pigeons, which I decided would be a novel way to send out the party invitations. We delivered the pigeons to the reporters and editors we were targeting, and they R.S.V.P.'d on a roll of paper in a capsule attached to the birds' feet and then released them out the window. One New York editor, however, messengered his pigeon back to me personally—dead—with a number two yellow pencil through its heart. Not a good omen.

But the party started off well enough, with a good crowd of style and beverage editors. We'd decided to have a contest to see who could find the best mixer for Crow Light, so we had a dozen bartenders with everything from grenadine to ice cream set up in a big reception area outside the ballroom. For an hour, the blenders whirled like mad, and everybody was happily shouting, "You try my drink, and I'll try yours," and getting pleasantly soused.

Prominent among this crowd was a writer for *Penthouse*, who showed up in a white suit with a Penthouse Pet on each arm. This guy was very taken with himself; and at some point, when he saw the crow on its trainer's arm, decided that he should be the one with the crow. He already had two Pets with him, but he insisted he had to have the crow.

The trainer resisted, so the writer decided to give me a hard time about it. Eventually, I said to the trainer, "Just give him the crow."

We watched this guy strut around for a moment with the bird on his shoulder, and then I said, "You know, I don't really care if we do get an article in *Penthouse*."

The trainer gave me a knowing look and immediately blew his little whistle. The crow did exactly what it was supposed to do, all over the guy's white suit. It was a beautiful moment. Even the Pets jumped away from him.

Eventually, after ingesting untold amounts of light whisky disguised by all kinds of mixers, the crowd moved in to dinner. It was my brilliant idea to prepare everything with Crow Light. We had a fruit cup. Instead of Kirsch, it was made with Crow Light. Instead of a wine vinaigrette for the salad dressing, it was a "lightaigrette" made with Crow Light. Instead of a marsala sauce, the veal had a Crow Light sauce. Even the dessert was made with Crow Light.

By the time the National Distillers marketing director got up to speak, people literally had their heads on the table. The poor guy was up there in his suit with his slides, marching through his presentation, and no one in a crowd of 150 was even capable of taking notes. A few reporters actually wound up with their faces in the Crow-Light-laced crème brulée.

The good news was, they all wrote glowing articles about Crow Light straight from our press releases. They couldn't remember enough and were too embarrassed to do anything else.

The bad news was, Crow Light was an utter failure, the Edsel of liquors. And introducing an offshoot that consumers despised did nothing to endear the original product, Old Crow Bourbon, to them.

What strategy should National Distillers have used to combat declining whisky sales? First, the company should have recognized that it was not confronting a momentary slump, but a sea change among consumers. Compromise was not possible, but a compromise was what they were trying to effect with this brand extension. The company had made a more intelligent investment a few years earlier when, instead of resisting the changing preferences of consumers, it had decided to go with the flow and buy a wine brand, Almaden.

Second, National Distillers should have paid much more attention to consumers' negative reactions to its product before releasing it. At the very least, it should not have given the stuff the Crow name. It was foolish to risk all the goodwill attached to a brand message that had taken years to create on an experimental product that tasted like . . . an experiment.

Of course, even more dangerous than a line extension is moving into a new business entirely, one you may know little about. Unfortunately, it is the easiest thing in the world to fantasize that your brand is omnipotent and that its best attributes would transform any business, and I'm not immune. At John Hancock, before we came to our senses, we once actually contemplated buying Brink's (the armored car business), on the theory that the trustworthiness Hancock enjoyed as an insurance brand would automatically transfer to a completely unrelated business. There ought to be a corporate firing squad for ideas like that.

The classic example of this kind of overreaching is Sears. Sears was America's biggest retailer in 1981 when it decided it was going to go into the financial services business in a big way. So it acquired the real estate broker Coldwell Banker and the brokerage house Dean Witter and added them to the auto and home insurer it had long owned, Allstate. Sears had a grand plan: People would not only buy their new refrigerator from America's number-one retailer; they'd find their new house there and get their mortgage and homeowner's insurance as well; and if they had anything left over, they'd invest that with Sears, too.

With its huge customer base, trusted brand, and large number of retail locations, it seemed as if Sears could not lose. The company set up financial boutiques in its stores for Dean Witter and Coldwell Banker and expected to cash in. And Sears' competitors within the financial services industry were duly frightened. The Chairman of Citicorp at the time sounded as if he thought Sears had so many advantages, the whole thing was no fair: "When you look at what Sears is doing," he said, "the question is whether commercial banks can compete."

What Sears neglected to determine before setting out on this odyssey was whether the company's brand really extended as far as financial services. It did not. Consumers did not necessarily transfer the trust they had for Sears as a peddler of power drills and lawn mowers to Sears as a peddler of stocks. And they were certainly not comfortable discussing their finances amidst the wrenches and dishwashers. The whole concept was kind of Orwellian. In the meantime, of course, as Sears built its financial empire, its attentions were divided, and the core retailing business began losing ground to tough competitors like Wal-Mart, ground that Sears has never recovered.

By the 1990s, Sears had realized its mistake and shed Allstate, Coldwell Banker, and Dean Witter. But a brand extension misadventure like this is not easily correctable, because a failure in the new line tends to penetrate and poison the core business. Those customers who have a bad experience with the new venture tend to hold it against the old business as well.

Of course, as foolish as it was of Sears to think that its trustworthy image would stretch from socks to stocks, there *are* brands whose messages hinge more upon an idea, a personality, or a method of distribution than they do a particular business. And in that case, an extension across unrelated businesses may actually work. British billionaire and Virgin Group founder Richard Branson offers an interesting example. He's put his Virgin brand, which started out as a record label, on everything from airlines to bridal wares to mobile phones to financial services.

And he's been more or less successful in keeping the Virgin brand intact through all this, because Virgin is not a *record* brand that's been extended to other businesses. Rather, it's a *Richard Branson* brand that he applies to any venture he fancies with the same irreverent spirit. And the people who work for him know it. Explaining the failure of Virgin Cola in the United States, one of Branson's executives told *Fortune* magazine, "The original management team made assumptions that the Virgin name and Branson persona were stronger here than they were."

In Virgin's case, I'd recommend that the sign in the office read, "The *persona*, stupid."

The question is, will Virgin be able to hold all these diverse businesses together under one brand message once Branson goes—or grows so long in the tooth that everyone forgets his boyish charm?

Maybe. Maybe not.

A certain amount of humility is in order when it comes to brand messages. They are not infinitely elastic. If you try to stretch them too far, they tend to unravel. And there is no question that consumers will hold it against your base business if you put your brand on a new business you turn out not to be very good at. No brand builder should consider stretching his or her brand message across a new product line without first thinking long and hard about whether the risk is worth it.

Ultimately, a strong brand message has a lot in common with a bucking bronco. It's not going to stand still for a second—it has to change constantly as the times and the competition do— but once you've managed to get on top of it, you do not want to let go. Lose your grip or fail to make the right adjustments when adjustments are in order, and watch your business be pitched into the sawdust. Better to hang on and ride that message to the applause of the crowd for as long and as stylishly as you can.

IF YOU WANT GREAT ADVERTISING, BE PREPARED TO FIGHT FOR IT

It's not enough just to know what your brand stands for. A brand has to be given a voice through its advertising. This is easier said than done. Consumers are bombarded by commercial messages and, by now, are almost immune to them. Only the most distinctive advertising gets through their radar.

Unfortunately, most advertising is the opposite of distinctive. Instead, it's a series of personality-free clichés. We've all channel-surfed past these ads: the financial services commercial with a bride coming down the stairs, the guests throwing rice, and a voiceover about planning for life's great moments; the car commercial with the vehicle careening around a mountain until it comes to a stop on a plateau; the cleaning product commercial with cartoon bunnies trundling along to some annoying jingle.

Instead of watching all this awful stuff for its content, I amuse myself by trying to imagine instead what the meeting was like when it was approved. Overwhelmingly, ineffective advertising has one source: badly managed relationships between the various agency and corporate players.

BEWARE OF FLATTERERS

One of the biggest mistakes you can make as a brand builder is to assume that advertising agencies want to help you build your brand and sell your products. Don't be silly; what they *really* want is to keep you as a fee-paying client for as long as possible. The general character of the advertising business is sycophancy. A lot of agencies will produce any nonsense you want, so long as it keeps you happy and you can pay for it.

Let me tell you a story that illustrates how advertising agencies often work. When I was in the advertising business in the early 1980s, the agency I worked for was trying to win the promotional business of the roofing division of Owens Corning. Owens Corning's fiberglass insulation division had recently launched its Pink Panther campaign, which continues to this day. The first time my partner Bob and I were sent to the company headquarters in Toledo, Ohio, it was immediately obvious to us that the roofing guys were viewed as second-class citizens. The truth is, a strong branding campaign like the Pink Panther works on the inside of a company, as well as on the outside. The guys associated with it—the insulation guys—were suddenly perceived to be the dynamic players, and were now first in line for all the top jobs.

The roofing guys were therefore eager for a promotional campaign that would put *them* on the map. Since this would generate, potentially, millions of dollars in fees for the agency, Bob and I were ordered to wage our own campaign to win the account.

So we went back to Toledo again and again. We ate dozens of flash-frozen, portion-controlled steaks in some of the worst restaurants I've ever set foot in. We spent uncounted hours listening to our potential clients prattle on about R-values (a measure, in case you happen not to be fixated on these questions, of a substance's ability to insulate). We sat forever on coffee shop stools shooting the breeze with Toledo natives, just to gain some insight into how the potential clients lived. And as a final test of our mettle, we agreed to share something very big in the prospective clients' lives: We went to New Orleans for the National Roofing Contractors Convention.

Let me tell you, you haven't lived until you've been to New Orleans in the middle of the sweltering summer for a roofing convention. We even attended the clients' party at the Marriott—a few hundred people and six shrimp in a ballroom the size of the *Queen Mary*. And yes, we did dance in a Pete Fountain-led conga line, groaning to ourselves, "God, what I'll do to make the rent."

The day after the big party, we were supposed to present our ideas to the clients' assembled regional vice presidents and other assorted players. So they set us up in this little meeting room with red flocked velvet wallpaper that looked like the anteroom of an 1890s New Orleans whorehouse. The presentation was one and one-half hours long, but it took 13 hours to finish it.

Why? Because they mistook us for a videotape playing on a continuous loop. Guys wandered in and out of the room all day long. There were always six or seven executives in there listening to us, but they were always different. If one wanted to go to the "Why the Sun Cracks Your Roof" seminar for awhile, he would leave and then return three hours later. One guy would say to the other, "Charlie, did you see this part already?"

And Charlie would inevitably reply, "No, let's go back to the beginning."

I felt like Howdy Doody, but since you never quite know who makes the decisions in these situations, I didn't dare quit.

At some point, as exhaustion threatened, Bob, who was much more tolerant than I was, told me, "David, forget all the statistics. Forget all the reasons this marketing makes sense. This is a presentation that will succeed on our ability to validate to these people who they are. So we're going to work from The Box."

Before we get to "The Box," I should say that all our research in Toledo convinced us that the best way to win the account was to be as homespun, as patriotic, and as Norman Rockwell as the potential clients seemed to be. So we settled on the slogan, "America, your roof is leaking"; decided that everything would be red, white, and blue; and what better idea than to use Norman Rockwell wherever we could? We designed a promotion around Rockwell's famous illustration of a baseball umpire putting his hand out to see if it's raining. If a contractor sent for a roofing brochure, he'd get a free, full-sized copy in return.

The heart of the campaign, however, was The Box. We proposed sending a package to thousands of roofing contractors, homebuilders, architects, and engineers all over the country. Naturally, The Box would contain brochures and samples, as well as a number of completely unnecessary things, such as an umbrella, a slide rule, a bucket, some sponges, and red-white-and-blue scarves embroidered with the phrase, "America, your roof is leaking."

It was a tchotchke campaign. And it was designed to do two things:

1. First, flatter the client and win the account. The other guys might have had the Pink Panther, but with The Box, we'd give the roofing guys an identity they could actually hold in their hands.

2. Second, generate the greatest possible amount of revenue for the agency. The agency made sure of that. The production department could have proposed a standard-sized box for this package. No, they decided on a custom-sized box, because the agency could make a lot more money off of it. In addition to the 15 percent the client would be charged on the entire package, the agency was going to take a huge markup on the printing and a huge markup on every single piece of junk that went inside.

So we worked from The Box. I sat down and Bob started pulling out the tchotchkes. He was heroic. In the 100-degree New Orleans weather, he put on the Owens Corning ski hat, scarf, and windbreaker. He threw the dry sponges with the Owens Corning logo on them into a bowl of water, and the logo ballooned up to full size. You should have heard the "oohs" and "aahhs" at that. He put the bucket on his head and did a little dance. He must have repeated this performance 10 or 20 times. (Remember, we were playing on a continuous loop.) I don't know if it was Bob's frivolity that tipped the balance or his endurance, but that day we won the account.

By our agency's standards, The Box was a huge success. The clients gave them away by the thousands. The agency made a fortune.

Then the most unexpected of all things happened: Sales went up. In the following weeks, we sold millions of dollars of commercial roofing materials and gave a substantial boost to Owens Corning as a roofing brand.

The campaign worked! But that was sheer coincidence.

You see, our agency had calculated going in that we would probably have this account only for a short period of time. Odds were, the insulation guys would soon win control of the company and its marketing and give our account to the agency that had come up with the Pink Panther idea for them. So the agency's goals for this multimillion-dollar campaign were to make the clients happy and make some fast money.

And if the campaign actually sold some roofing at the same time, well, no one was more astonished than we were.

You know, this account really taught me a lot about the advertising business—mainly, that this was *not* a business I wanted to be in. I left advertising soon afterward.

Of course, the joke wound up being on *us*, the supposedly shrewd advertising pros. It turned out that the Owens Corning people actually understood their potential markets pretty well.

The things we proposed in an attempt to flatter them actually worked with the people to whom they were selling. But, often, advertising clients aren't so lucky. And they allow fee-hungry agencies to talk them into campaigns that do nothing for their brands or their bottom line.

Naturally, you might assume that my former employer represented a particularly diabolical brand of advertising agency. Well, keep this in mind: The advertising business is brutal. The agencies are completely dependent on their clients, and the clients are not necessarily terribly loyal. According to the American Association of Advertising Agencies, the average length of time a client stays with an agency declined more than 25 percent between 1985 and 1997, from 7.2 to 5.3 years. Survival in the advertising game demands that the agencies learn how to flatter and milk their clients.

And lest we paint the entire advertising profession as a society of opportunists, we'd better establish one thing: Advertising professionals arrive at this advanced state of cynicism only after their clients drive them to it.

IT'S NOT NECESSARILY GOOD ADVERTISING THAT THE CLIENT IS AFTER

Most advertising agencies think their clients are fools, and, unfortunately, the clients give them ample reason to feel that way. For example, years ago, the agency I was with had as a client a prominent national brand. We were looking for a model for a television and print campaign for this company. The type we needed was somebody in her early twenties with a Rebecca of Sunnybrook Farm look—a slightly freckled, refreshing strawberry blonde. The director of the commercials, the agency creative director, and I worked hard to find just the right face and personality. We'd searched through hundreds of portfolios, had screen-tested dozens of wholesome beauties, and had finally narrowed the list to a couple of young actresses, when my boss walked in and said, "By the way, we've got the girl for the commercials."

Then he showed me a portfolio of a woman who was clearly pushing 40 and was a brunette at best. It wasn't clear that she'd *ever* been to Sunnybrook Farm, and she certainly hadn't been there in the past 15 years, at least. I couldn't figure it out. Using this woman would be like making a commercial about cat food, featuring camels. It made no sense.

It turned out, naturally, that the actress in question was the girlfriend of the client, and she had a history of appearing in that company's promotions.

Here I'd bonded with the creative people over the search for just the right face for the campaign, and now it was my job to convince them to accept an unacceptable, ahem, "model." At that point, they just shut down creatively. They shot the commercials robotically, took the money, and couldn't care less about the results.

The client was happy. His girlfriend was happy, too. But I doubt very much if the end product of that multimillion-dollar effort ever sold a penny's worth of product.

CLIENTS MAY BE DOING SOME SUCKING UP OF THEIR OWN

Of course, there are dozens of other agendas clients have besides just pleasing the girlfriend that can ruin an advertising campaign. The advertising John Hancock did just before I arrived at the company offers a slightly different example.

It took weeks before the agency would deign to let me see the rough-cuts of the commercials they'd just made. It was the usual prattle that you see from financial services companies: the Ozzie and Harriet family stuff, the father praising the boy who has just gotten into college, and the little girl announcing that her braces would soon be coming off. It was remarkably forgettable, but what I do remember is its peculiar theme: scales. The family sat on one side of the scales, and then brass weights representing John Hancock products descended onto the other side as a voice-over said, "Thanks to John Hancock, you can balance your needs for the future."

I couldn't figure out how the agency had arrived at anything so dumb until one day I was in the then-president's office, which is now my office. He had a set of built-in glass shelves that faced his desk. I'd never looked around the corner at what was on them, but on this particular day, I stuck my head around. Sure enough, the shelves were full of antique scales. He liked collecting antique scales.

I suddenly had a sneaking suspicion. I certainly could have been wrong, but did some of the advertising people actually think they could protect their budget, their influence, and their jobs against interference from me—the new guy—by appealing to the president's *hobby*?

Actually, they had been very clever; when people assumed that this awful campaign was the president's idea, nothing was done to dissuade them. People were afraid even to *object* to these dumb commercials. No one was willing to tell the emperor that he had no clothes. Of course, things could have been worse; the boss could have collected shrunken heads instead, and then we would have had shrunken-head commercials.

The president, of course, had no idea that people were using our advertising to suck up to him, and he quickly allowed me to make sure that the campaign was short-lived.

THE CLIENT MAKES A BIG IDEA SMALL

Peculiar agendas are common enough in advertising, but by far the most common thing clients do to destroy their own advertising is to allow little minds to improve it.

For all the bad things I've said about advertising agencies, the truth is that the people on the creative side will take their very best shot at doing something unique and different for you the first time around. No matter how dismal the final product turns out to be, I always assume that the first time the commercial was presented in storyboard form, it was actually excellent. It had crisp language, good music, and appropriate silences. It had a strong visual style. It had purity. It was the unfettered product of two talented people: the art director and the copywriter.

And probably, having done their absolute best, these creative people went to a meeting with the client, only to hear how
wonderful their idea was. Clients always say how wonderful the
idea is initially, because they like to think of themselves as the
kind of people who are sensitive to the creative process. So the
creatives will sit there, buoyed, thinking, "They love my concept, my music, my art." They feel validated. And then, about
a day later it begins: the gradual tearing down that sends advertising pros to rubber rooms with such frequency. First, the
account executive gets a call from the advertising manager at
the client's company. "You know," he or she says, "I was thinking about those commercials last night, and I'm not a creative
person, but . . . ."

That's a great line: "I'm not a creative person, but . . . ." It
should immediately disqualify anybody who uses it from having
anything to do with the advertising. And then, he or she gets to
the point: "Could we change the baby to a miniature schnauzer?"

It only gets worse. Next, the corporate marketing director
gets hold of the commercials and is incensed that there is no
scene in which the product is featured. Most amateurs think that
because they're paying for the airtime, every second of a commercial has to be occupied, preferably with as many mentions
of the company's products as possible. So now the creatives have
to make the miniature schnauzer interact with the product.

Next, a dumb jingle is added, because the president of the
division takes it home to his wife and she says, "This would be
great if it ended with a song."

Then, of course, the various attorneys get involved and make
their contributions to the inane mess: "We can't use a miniature

schnauzer because schnauzer fanciers are very militant. In all like-lihood, they'll sue. Besides, I think bulldogs are funnier anyway." I have yet to meet a lawyer who, when he sees a piece of advertising copy, doesn't add a creative idea. And if the company is a start-up, there may well be a know-nothing from the venture capital firm contributing his or her ideas. Finally, if the creatives try to resist any of this, there are always their friends at the agency—the account executive and the agency head—to emasculate them by reminding them that money is all that matters.

So what started out as a beautiful piece of veal is now a much less distinguished stew. And any brand builder who allows this kind of mass cookery to go on will find that the next campaign will be even worse. You've ruined the creative people, taken away their options. You know what? Next time, they don't want to work that hard for you. To them, it's like flipping burgers now.

Here is the great tragedy of the advertising professional: Advertising is like sports. You don't have to know much to sound authoritative about it: "Jeez, did you see that game last night? Hell of a play, wasn't it?" So a lot of people who know nothing somehow feel completely qualified to override the ideas of people who spend their lives writing, designing, casting, and directing advertising.

The truth is, there are reasons people wind up as creatives in advertising agencies. They're short of being filmmakers and poets; but they're way, way ahead of being corporate marketing people. Yet, the creatives are always forced to defer to the marketing people on the work they understand best.

It is maddening for them. That is why so many advertising pros turn to drugs and drink and other means of obliterating the absurdities of life.

One of the first people I worked with in New York was an alcoholic, like a lot of people in advertising and public relations who came out of the 1960s. By the time I met him, he was in his mid-forties, burnt out and beaten up by clients and by his bosses. He was brilliant, but his ideas had been destroyed once too often, and he didn't care about being original any more. What he cared about was getting by. Every morning around 10 o'clock, we'd go out for a "popsicle," which was a double vodka on the rocks. If he had 10 or 12 of those a day, it was a slow day.

It was a wonderful exchange for me. He needed a young person with energy to cover for him. So he basically turned over his accounts to me. In turn, he protected me within the organization and allowed me to learn the business incredibly fast. When young people say to me, "What's the key to success?" I always say, "Go to a big city and sign on with a brilliant addict."

The good news is, there is no shortage of them in any creative field. The bad news is, you may not get a positive reaction if you decide to ask your potential employer about his or her substance abuse problems in the middle of a job interview.

DO NOT ALLOW THE ADVERTISING TO BE HIT ON

What, on the other hand, is the key to great advertising?

Simple! Do not be a party to this human wreckage.

Do not allow people who have no business having anything to do with the advertising to hit on it. Twenty-two people cannot create a single, clear message for a brand. Here's my rule of thumb: If you find that more than three people in the company have "improved" a commercial, throw it out.

The way you produce advertising that sets your brand apart is you let the creatives do their thing. When it comes to the advertising, the brand builder's most important job is to protect the creatives at all costs, so long as they stay true to the brand.

In early 1986, after we'd gotten rid of the agency that made those infamous commercials with the scales, John Hancock began a long-running campaign called "Real Life, Real Answers." These commercials not only won the highest awards, including best campaign at both the Clio Awards and at the Cannes Film Festival, but they were so unusual in their realism and so touching, that people still remember them to this day.

One called "Michael Mark" had a sobering effect on a generation of yuppies. People tell me they still remember, even 15 years later, the older brother in the spot shaming his younger brother with "Are you making 30 now?" and telling him it was time to stop pretending he was 18 and start putting some of it away. Other commercials in the campaign were more overtly emotional, such as one that featured a football player announcing his retirement. Choking back tears, he says that he wants to be remembered as a good husband and father, because that's all life is.

These were little 30-second dramas, the turning points in particular lives, intercut with black-and-white art cards that silently gave the relevant facts: the names of the protagonists, their incomes, the products they needed, and then John Hancock's logo at the end. There were no jingles—nothing but ambient noise and the sound of very real-seeming people expressing their fears and hopes. There were no helicopter shots, just a camera close enough to these people to establish an incredible sense of intimacy with them. These were completely unlike any financial services commercials ever produced. We were not bragging about ourselves—there was no comparing the company to a big mountain or a crashing sea. Instead, the tone was humble. We were that invisible fly on the wall, eavesdropping on our customers to learn about their concerns.

These commercials did something far more important than tell people we sold life insurance and mutual funds. Instead, they perfectly captured the empathetic nature of the John Hancock brand, helped to deepen it, and gave consumers a reason to choose us instead of our competitors.

They demonstrated that we understood how people actually live, and they brought many new customers to our doors. Think about it. Would you be more inclined to buy life insurance from a company whose advertising tells you it understands you or from a company that has a cartoon character telling you what to buy? In 1986, the first year of the campaign, our life insurance sales rose 17 percent, while the sales of life insurance industry-wide grew only a dismal 1 percent.

The key to getting those commercials made was, of course, the brilliance of the creative team at our agency—Hill, Holliday, Connors, Cosmopulos—and, on the John Hancock side, a steadfast refusal to allow anybody who didn't belong there to insert himself or herself into the creative process. We never even showed the spots to the lawyers or John Hancock's top executives until they were complete.

It's not easy to shoo powerful people away from the advertising. Do it anyway.

Even though noses will be out of joint in the short term, in the long term you have nothing to lose by being a bully on this score. The advertising is guaranteed to be awful if a lot of people hit on it, and then it will be *your* fault. When it's successful, no one will even remember how stubborn you were, because they'll all be so busy taking credit for your success.

BE MEMORABLE

When John Hancock was developing the "Real Life, Real Answers" campaign, we told the creative team that we didn't want to see anything except something directly from their own lives.

They said, "Why?"

We said, "Because otherwise you cannot truly feel it." We wanted these commercials to stand out because of the reality of their emotion.

So the creative team did what we wanted. The first spot we produced featured an ordinary guy named Bill Heater carrying a newborn baby named Jenny Katherine, telling her that Daddy got a raise and asking her advice on how they ought to spend it. It was intimate, charming, touching, and completely different in style from anything any other financial services company had ever done. The copywriter? A brilliant guy named Bill Heater who'd just had a real baby named Jenny Katherine. I don't think it's any coincidence that this was the spot that carried off the Grand Prix at Cannes.

Of course, every time an advertising agency sells another client on the familiar wedding commercial, with the bride being pelted by rice, the agency argues, "It's a special moment, a slice of life." Actually, it's a slice of olestra, so generic and sanitized that it cannot hope to command the attention of jaded consumers.

Advertising must be memorable to succeed. Fortunately, there are an infinite number of ways to achieve memorability. "Real Life, Real Answers" was memorable for its unadorned reality. Our next campaign, on the other hand, was memorable instead for its poetry—for its striking black-and-white photography, poignant Irish music, and copywriting that managed to discuss consumers' financial fears in language that aspired to Yeats.

But no matter what your stylistic choices, you will never be memorable if you cannot understand that we don't all lead lives in which rice is being thrown at the wedding. Most companies are afraid to produce advertising that suggests anything unpleasant. They give consumers no credit for any intelligence or maturity and think it's better to tell them soothing lies than to capture the true flavor of their lives. That is why so much advertising is just a blur.

At John Hancock, we've managed to distinguish ourselves with our willingness to call it the way it is.

We are not afraid to do commercials that are extremely sad. We did one set in a college dorm room in which a middle-aged man with a terminal illness tries to reassure his son that everything will be okay financially, and the boy sobs silently.

We are also not afraid of stirring up trouble. We did a commercial that featured a teary woman in a phone booth talking, obviously, to her louse of an ex-husband, who'd forgotten to call their son on his birthday. Our salespeople thought it was an abomination. We got hundreds of calls from divorced dads who were furious at being portrayed as deadbeats. So what did we do? We ran the spot more often. We knew people were watching.

Another, more recent spot features a man visiting his ex-wife and announcing that he's moving away with his girlfriend, leaving the responsibility of raising their son entirely to her. It shows something extremely unusual in advertising: a genuine moment of anger. And you know what? With divorce rates that suggest that nearly half of all American marriages will eventually break up, it's a good bet that the audience is ready not only to comprehend such a commercial, but also to identify with it.

Great advertising takes something rare in business: courage. If it helps you cut through the clutter and tell the story of your brand, don't be afraid of controversy.

And don't feel that you will alienate a large percentage of your audience if you decide to talk about a small portion of it. In 2000, John Hancock did a commercial that generated a lot of interest and controversy because it showed two women bringing an adopted baby home from Asia. They might be gay, though the spot doesn't force the idea on you. They might be sisters instead. And it's just dawning on them that life will never be the same. Of course, we could have shot the cliché instead—the new dad peering into the bassinet, feeling the awesome financial responsibility—but not a single person outside the company would have paid any attention at all to that spot.

You might assume that what John Hancock does is targeted advertising—advertising aimed at specific demographic groups:

gay women, divorced moms, or single guys burning through their paychecks too fast. It's not. There has never been anything segmented about our advertising, unlike a lot of stuff I've been seeing lately that has, for example, "We are now going after aging boomers" written all over it. Who cares who the company is going after? All that stuff is a blur for consumers anyway, who are merely looking to be amused or moved by what they see and who actually are quite capable of understanding lives different from their own.

No matter what the particular scenario shown in any John Hancock commercial, we think the audience at large will find something to recognize in it and say, "Gee, that's like someone I know. This brand understands modern life."

Although we seek to give every commercial a distinct flavor, ultimately our commercials are not about the specific circumstances depicted in them. We are not saying, "If you're a lesbian about to adopt a child, you need our products." We're saying something much bigger: "Whoever you are, we'll go out of our way to understand your concerns."

DON'T CHANGE THE ADVERTISING BECAUSE YOU'RE BORED WITH IT

No matter how successful their advertising is, some companies seem to change to a new campaign every eight or nine months. There are a lot of forces weighing in on the side of upheaval. The advertising agencies are always pushing for fresh campaigns because they are a source of new revenue for them. A new corporate advertising director always wants to change everything because he or she wants to put his or her imprint on it. And finally, everybody inside the company eventually gets tired of the advertising.

But that doesn't mean that the public is tired of it. In fact, if your campaign is successful, people actually look forward to seeing the next commercial in it, as if the commercial were the next installment in a soap opera. This is the best of all possible scenarios for your brand, and the smart brand builder will think long and hard before giving up that kind of attachment.

At John Hancock, we stayed true to our "Real Life, Real Answers" format despite enormous pressure to change, until the format itself was widely copied. And though we've done two major campaigns since, our voice is unchanged. A John Hancock commercial shown yesterday is still recognizably similar in tone to one that aired 15 years ago. We're not telling the story of our products through our advertising, because the products tend to change with the times. We're telling the story of our brand; and thanks to the quality of the work done by our advertising agency, that story is getting richer over the years.

I don't mean to make any of this sound easy. Advertising is the most artistic of all corporate endeavors. As with any artistic pursuit, you cannot dictate that the end result be great. The best thing you can do is establish the conditions that allow for greatness. For the brand builder, that means, first, understanding what your brand stands for and conveying it to the creative people who will write and design your advertising. And then, giving them the freedom to express it.

Want to make memorable advertising? The rule is, be a great client. Don't interfere unnecessarily, and don't allow anyone else to interfere. Protect the creatives, and you'll soon have the best copywriters and art directors in the world clamoring to work for you, and great work will follow of its own accord.

5

WHEN IT COMES TO SPONSORSHIPS, THERE'S A SUCKER BORN EVERY 30 SECONDS

However crucial advertising is, it has one severe limitation as a brand-building tool: You are asking something of consumers—that they pay attention to your message and buy your products—without giving them very much in return.

Sponsorships, on the other hand, offer consumers a much more even exchange. Yes, they have to put up with you as a commercial presence. But in return, you bring them something that they might not have otherwise seen, such as a sporting event or concert, a charitable venture, or the performance of an athlete who might not have been able to train without your support. By contributing to something consumers value, you may win their interest and respect, perhaps even their gratitude. Ideally, they see the glamour, excitement, and emotion of the event or person you are sponsoring as attributes of your brand as well.

This transfer of emotion from an event or person to the sponsoring brand is often called a "halo effect," and many big and powerful brands got that way because they managed to snag such halos. Nike, of course, offers one of the great examples of the halo effect in the history of business. By tying itself so closely to athletes like Tiger Woods and Michael Jordan, the Nike brand took on their air of cool mastery to dominate the sports apparel world. But other brands have also made brilliant use of the halo. Ben & Jerry's, for example, has used its support for environmental and social causes to give its brand a caring voice and distinguish itself from its faceless competition in the freezer case. And through its long-running partnership with the Olympic Games—the most desirable ticket in the world of sports—Visa has vividly demonstrated to consumers that it's everywhere they want to be, and has increased its market share from 40 to 53 percent.

Some corporations believe so devoutly in the halo effect that they try to literally grab a halo, as did the dozen big brands ranging from Mercedes-Benz to Ruffles potato chips that sponsored the Pope's 1998 visit to Mexico. Whether the commemorative picture of John Paul II in every bag boosted sales of Ruffles, I can't say. I suspect this cobranding opportunity didn't do much for the Catholic Church.

However, there is no question that a well-chosen and well-managed sponsorship can move your brand forward more dramatically than almost any other marketing activity, which explains why sponsorship is growing faster than any other form of marketing activity. According to IEG, the Chicago-based organization that monitors corporate sponsorships, spending on sponsorship fees in North America grew from $1 billion in 1985 to $8.7 billion in 2000.

There are other advantages to sponsorships besides the halo they can lend your brand. Sponsorships can be more cost-efficient than the purchase of advertising time or space, since they may generate a great deal of publicity for relatively little money. They can be enormously valuable just for the opportunity they give you to entertain your best clients and employees at a desirable event. And a well-managed sponsorship can bring coherence to your entire marketing program.

However, no brand builder should mistake any sponsorship for an automatic score. Sponsorships are essentially risky. So long as there is a potential halo effect, there is also a potential horn effect. If the person, group, or event you sponsor does something that makes consumers cringe, your brand may also make them cringe by association. Just ask Hertz, for example, whether it's really happy that it associated its brand so closely in consumers' minds with a charming former football player named O. J. Simpson, or ask Pepsi how it feels about its formerly close relationship with Michael Jackson, who was accused of child molestation in the middle of a Pepsi-sponsored tour.

There are dangers, as John Hancock has learned, in marrying your brand to even the purest of events. After five years of reaping the benefits from our status as one of less than a dozen worldwide Olympic sponsors, we woke up one morning in late 1998 to discover we were now linked with a situation that represented the opposite of integrity. Stories coming out of Salt Lake City, the host city of the 2002 Winter Olympic Games, revealed that there were some people at the International Olympic Committee (IOC) who apparently traveled the globe extorting cash, jewelry, tuition fees, you name it, from cities hoping to host the Games. To say we were unhappy about this development is to understate the case, and we believe that if the scandal had gone on too long without a resolution, it might very well have hurt our brand.

What's more, the potential pitfalls of sponsorships are by no means limited to scandal. Ambush—a marketing ploy in which your competitors pretend to be sponsors without paying for the sponsorship—is a perennial annoyance at the biggest events. Until Nike finally went legit and took over Reebok's spot as an official sponsor of the 2000 Olympic Games, it was a notorious pirate. During the 1996 Olympic Games in Atlanta, Nike stole Reebok's thunder by shoeing some of the most prominent athletes, by creating a giant Nike exhibit in a parking garage next to the Centennial Olympic Park, and by running Olympic-themed television commercials, including one unforgettably aggressive spot that declared, "You don't win silver, you lose gold."

Officially sanctioned ambush, otherwise known as clutter, is also an increasing problem. The NFL, for example, went from selling just eight major sponsorships a few years ago to selling 30 or more today. It's very hard to stand out in that crowd. There may be so many sponsors for a given event that your brand's presence there is simply ignored, and the millions you paid to be involved are thoroughly wasted.

At John Hancock, we believe that the potential rewards of sponsorship can be very great. We're not just a top Olympic sponsor, but also a major sponsor of Major League Baseball, the Boston Marathon, the Champions on Ice figure-skating tour, and other sports and philanthropic ventures. But we've also learned through painful experience the true nature of the sponsorship business, which is *buyer beware*.

The truth is, many corporations embarking on their first sponsorships behave like Little Red Riding Hood on her way to Grandma's house. They're so trusting and so excited about the trip that they can't tell the difference between Grandma and a wolf. Well, some of the toughest, most unscrupulous, desperate, and dangerous people you'll ever meet adhere to the worlds of sports and entertainment. Any brand builder planning on doing business with them had better be equally tough in return.

FIRST OF ALL, GET IN FOR THE RIGHT REASONS

The first step toward a successful sponsorship is making sure you're getting in for the right reasons. Many—maybe even most—sponsors don't.

When I was in the advertising business, I once tried to get a banking client to sponsor college football, which was rising in popularity at the time. The client actually looked at me and said, "Why would anyone worthwhile watch football on a Saturday afternoon, when he or she could watch polo instead?" So we brought him a polo proposal, and he liked that. Never mind that only a minuscule portion of his customers had even heard of polo and that the sponsorship therefore did him little good. Sponsoring it made him a player in his own mind.

The world of sports is incredibly seductive to graying executives, who often would like nothing better than to recapture the days when they were jocks or dreamed of being jocks. And far too often, the CEO or the brand builder signs on to a sport largely because he or she has some affection for it, and not because it will make a bit of difference to his or her potential customers.

The classic example of a sponsorship designed to buoy the corporate ego more than the brand is golf. Between 1989 and 1999, despite the advent of Tiger Woods, the PGA's average television ratings fell 19 percent, while the cost of reaching a thousand households rose 71 percent.

The theory behind golf as a sponsorship is that you use it to reach a limited, but upscale audience of consumers, or if you are a business-to-business brand, to entertain your best clients. What's surprising, however, is the number of golf sponsorships purchased by consumer-product brands that are not particularly upscale and not striving to be.

Let's be honest here. Many companies are in the sport primarily because the CEO is dying to be in the Pro-Am with Tiger Woods. That can quickly become one expensive round of golf.

Even worse are those ego-driven sponsorships that represent potential disaster for a brand. One sponsorship that always struck me as particularly wrong-headed was Virgin Group founder Richard Branson's jaunts in a balloon with a giant Virgin logo on it. Branson spent a few years attempting to be the first person to circle the globe in a balloon, calling it "the last great aviation record and adventure left on earth," before finally being beaten by another team.

This kind of ballooning is incredibly dangerous. In his career, Branson bailed into the icy waters off of Scotland, crash-landed on a frozen lake in the Canadian wilderness, and nearly plummeted into the Saharan Atlas Mountains.

I freely admit that Branson's personal sense of daring is part of what makes the Virgin brand appealing. Here's the problem, though: The Virgin Group owns two airlines, Virgin Atlantic Airways and Virgin Express. As thrilling as ballooning might have been for Branson, it made no sense for his brand to be associated with things that kept crashing. After all, if you can't fly a balloon, what's the confidence that you can fly an airplane?

My advice is to think twice before spending millions of marketing dollars to flatter your CEO. In the long run, it tends not to be a smart career move. Inevitably, the boss is going to ask you how much sales revenue *your* expensive sports marketing program has generated. And most bosses will not consider the following line a satisfactory response: "Well, it hasn't generated any revenue, but *you*, sir, had a great time being a bigshot at the event."

UNDERSTAND THE PLAYERS

After you've determined that you have the right motives for stepping into the shark tank, make sure you know what to expect from the sharks. The key players in any potential sponsorship are the event organizer, the television network that will broadcast the event, possibly athletes or celebrities and their agents, and, of course, you, the innocent brand builder with your wagon load of cash.

The biggest mistake you can make is to assume that the other players have the same aims and interests as you do. In fact, their goals may be diametrically opposed to yours.

THE EVENT ORGANIZER

Event organizers would generally prefer to do without sponsors if the cost of putting on a show or a game were not so high. Since they are forced to seek your support, their goals are exactly the same as those of a college-aged son: They want to get as much money out of you as possible with as little contact as you'll permit. They'd prefer that you behave like an anonymous donor, not a member of the family.

Understanding this mindset can be a huge advantage. In 1986, for example, John Hancock was able to woo the Boston Marathon away from a number of very big brands, including McDonald's, Coors, and Mercedes-Benz, because we were able to guess the deepest wish of the event organizer, the Boston Athletic Association (BAA). It was for a philanthropist to appear with a check and save their proud old race from the unsavory commercial interests clamoring to ruin it.

Of course, they needed a sponsor desperately; the world's best runners were increasingly refusing to run the Boston Marathon, because there was no prize money attached to the race. But that didn't mean the BAA liked the prospect. So John

Hancock decided to behave less like an unsavory commercial interest than some of the other companies vying for the race. We didn't ask to put our name on it and turn it into the John Hancock Boston Marathon. We made a 10-year promise of support to the BAA, since renewed, so that they could plan for the future. We assured them we would not plaster our logo all over the course.

This quiet approach actually turned out to be the right decision from a brand standpoint. John Hancock has received endless praise in the press for its class and restraint. But there *are* limits to our delicacy. At the end of the negotiation for our sponsorship, we asked to see the Boston Marathon course, only to learn that it ended in front of the Prudential Center in Boston's Back Bay. At the time, Prudential was our biggest competitor.

Our position was clear: Move the finish line.

The BAA's response was, "How could we move the finish line?" The race had traditionally started on a hill in Hopkinton. The course had been carefully designed to mimic the topography of the original marathon course in Athens, and the Prudential Center was exactly 26 miles, 385 yards from that hill.

We said, "Well, then, we're not going to give you $10 million and save your race."

They were shocked to learn that this was so important to us. But once they understood that we were not about to spend millions of the company's money to provide free publicity to a competitor, they rethought the course, took a loop out of it, and found a way to have the race end at Copley Plaza, near our headquarters. And since then, the BAA has been extremely gracious, welcoming not just our dollars, but also our ideas for marketing the race, which quickly returned to its place as the greatest marathon in the world.

Not every event organizer, however, will deal as politely with your concerns as the BAA. For example, John Hancock was one of the first corporations in the late 1980s to become title sponsor of a college football game. It was called the "John Hancock Sun Bowl," and we'd paid a considerable sum of money for the title rights. The problem was, we were not getting the editorial mentions we wanted out of the deal, because the newspapers and broadcasters continued to call the game the "Sun Bowl." In fact, the editors at the Associated Press told us frankly that they would not give the game a commercial name if they could avoid it, and they would certainly never use our name in a headline.

After three years of failing to get any value from our title sponsorship, we went back to the Bowl Committee and asked them to help us by simply calling the game the "John Hancock Bowl."

"Why would we do that?" they asked.

"Because we're a valued sponsor, and we're not getting what we've paid for," proved not to be a compelling argument with these people.

Exasperated, I decided to speak in a language they understood. "Because I'll give you $50,000 a letter to drop the word 'Sun.'"

Gee, that worked! And the press was then forced to use our name.

Of course, our negotiations with the BAA and the Sun Bowl Committee now seem quaint compared to the difficulties of negotiating an advantageous deal today. As the costs of players' salaries and venues have risen for event organizers, they are more and more determined to wring as much as they can out of their corporate partners.

Since exclusivity is the key to a sponsorship (you use it to build an image that's different from that of your competitors), event organizers generally sell only one sponsorship per business category. A big event might have as sponsors one car brand, one beer brand, one snack food brand, etc. But the more money it takes to launch an event, the more narrowly event organizers define these categories, so, if necessary, they can sell a sponsorship to your competitor while claiming it is not a competitor at all. As an Olympic official once said to me, "The more pressure there is for us to make money, the thinner we slice the apple."

This leads to some surreal semantic situations, on the level of President Clinton's finessing the meaning of the word "is" during the Monica Lewinsky scandal. We once sat in a room with people from the U.S. Olympic Committee and had them tell us that John Hancock was not really in the life insurance business the way we think we are, because they had another life insurer they'd like to introduce as a sponsor.

We actually had to debate the nature of the Internet with Major League Baseball. They tried to tell us that the Internet was not part of our deal because it was really just a geographical territory, and we'd purchased exclusive rights to a different territory: the domestic United States. We pointed out that we considered it not a region, but a *vehicle for commerce*, and we would highly resent their selling the Internet rights to baseball to another financial services company.

Do not allow your exclusivity to be attacked. And do not assume you have absolute exclusivity just because the event organizer offers you some casual, verbal assurance that you do. The quality of the lying in the sports world surpasses even the lying in politics. It's practically Hollywoodesque. My advice is, get it in writing.

The truth is, in the sponsorship world, you frequently find that the people you've bought your exclusivity from are the first in line to compromise it. For example, during the Atlanta Olympic Games, despite the tens of millions of dollars we'd paid to the IOC for the right to be the exclusive Olympic life insurance sponsor worldwide, the Atlanta organizing committee (ACOG) suddenly discovered a loophole that would allow it to stick us up for even more money. That loophole was the space above our heads, the rights to which happened not to be spelled out in the sponsors' contracts. ACOG suddenly demanded several hundred thousand dollars from us if we wanted to hang John Hancock banners on streetlights.

As marketing devices, these banners were practically worthless, but ACOG knew that the sponsors would be bringing their boards of directors, their top clients, and their best salespeople to Atlanta for the Games. ACOG also knew they would not enjoy having to explain to these people why every other sponsor's name was overhead, but not theirs.

At John Hancock, however, we don't believe in buying defensively, and we don't enjoy being held up by the people we support. So, we turned down ACOG's offer. There were, however, less experienced sponsors in Atlanta who *did* allow themselves to be taken advantage of in this way.

Of course, of all event organizers, the local Olympic organizing committees may be the trickiest to deal with, because by the time you're ready to turn around and demand redress from them for breaching your sponsorship contract, the Games are over and the committees have gone out of existence.

Given what we had learned in Atlanta, I decided to share my hard-earned wisdom with the Australian companies that had signed on for the 2000 Games. I gave a speech in Sydney in 1997 advising them that if they discovered the Sydney organizing committee (SOCOG) violating the spirit of their contracts, they should sue early, sue often, and sue for damages.

People reacted as if I were attacking motherhood and apple pie. The audience was very upset with me, particularly the people from Channel 7, the official Australian broadcaster of the Sydney Games. Two years later, Channel 7 learned that SOCOG had secretly set aside hundreds of thousands of premium tickets and was offering them to nonsponsor corporations, devaluing one of the main advantages of sponsorship—the fact that you have access to great tickets and your competitors do not. Worse, SOCOG had sold a corporate suite at the main stadium to Kerry Packer, the owner of Channel 7's rival, the Nine Network.

Channel 7's response? It threatened to sue. Gee.

By all means, look for sponsorships with event organizers with whom you believe you can have a good relationship, but be realistic. You're likely to be adversaries as much as partners. Be tough, or be prepared to be gouged.

THE TELEVISION NETWORKS

If you're going to embark on any major sports sponsorship, the second group of players you'll have to understand is the television networks. And the most important thing to understand about them is that they are under siege. Thanks to the advent of umpteen cable and satellite channels, the prime-time audience share of the big three networks—ABC, NBC, and CBS—declined from 94 percent in 1955 to just 45 percent by 1999.

The networks desperately need sports programming in order to stay relevant to their audience and to promote their prime–time shows, and are keenly aware of how high the stakes are. When Fox outbid CBS in 1993 for football, for example, CBS lost the chance to advertise its prime–time shows during the game. In the first three years CBS was without the NFL, its prime-time ratings sank from 11.8 to 9.6, while Fox's prime-time ratings rose from 7.2 to 7.7.

This ferocious competition between television outlets has made one thing a reasonable bet: Whatever sports property you're thinking of sponsoring, the network has probably overpaid for it. For example, when the broadcast rights for pro football came up for negotiation in 1998, Disney, CBS, and Fox together paid a phenomenal $17.6 billion to run the games through 2005. The magazine *Sports Sense* calculated that the networks could have bought the entire National Football League outright for less money, a bargain at just $6.1 billion.

As a result of the huge rights fees they're paying, the networks are ruthless about recouping their costs. That means that you, the sponsor, can expect to have to crawl out from under some really astonishing clutter in order to be heard at all. For example, after the rights negotiation in 1998, the NFL allowed the networks to sell even more commercials during each game: a total of 59, up from an already mind-numbing 56. And the biggest contributor to advertising clutter on a sports broadcast may well be the network itself. On its broadcast of the Sydney Olympic Games in 2000, NBC ran an outrageous 639 commercials plugging its own shows.

The network's intense need to recoup its rights fees also means that when you're negotiating for your own advertising time, you'll be regarded the same way a particularly plump and juicy captive is regarded by your average cannibal. That is not to say that the network won't give you some very valuable things as a sponsor. You'll get first dibs on the advertising time during the game, and probably free time if the game runs into overtime. And there are a lot of other subtly advantageous things that may happen to you. The announcers may use your name if you're an official sponsor. If you have signage in the stadium, the cameramen may pan toward it and avoid your competitors' signage.

But expect the network also to practice a very unpleasant form of extortion, which it, of course, calls a "business necessity." Like an event organizer, the network creates categories for various businesses and assigns an arbitrary figure to these categories as the price of exclusivity. For the Olympics, for example, the network might ask for as much as $60 million if you'd like to be the sole advertiser in your business category for the Games broadcast.

What if you can't afford to buy $60 million worth of advertising time? At John Hancock, for example, $60 million is about three times our annual advertising budget. What if you only want to buy $20 million worth of commercial time? Well, the network immediately offers the $40 million of remaining time to your biggest competitors. It's that simple.

This is not a terribly polite negotiation, either. The networks generally give you 30 days to make up your mind; and they let you know that if you don't buy in, well, they've already got your competitors lined up and waiting. Presumably, since your competitors haven't already spent many millions of dollars to be the official sponsor, they'll have the cash to buy in. And the truth is, the average American on his or her couch lazily watching these competing commercials is unlikely to notice who's "official" and who is not.

Just to avoid this scenario, many sponsors wind up wasting unbelievable amounts of money on advertising time they don't need. Sports marketing is a high-testosterone endeavor, and senior marketing executives don't want the CEO embarrassed by any form of ambush. So often, the event turns into a spending frenzy to make the boss feel good that does nothing to make consumers feel better about your brand.

What can you do about it? First, don't make the networks any richer than they need to be just because you fear being emasculated through ambush. It takes discipline and guts to say "No." However, buy only the commercial time you need to buy to move your audience. Any more than that is just wasted.

Instead, rely on the brilliance of the creative content of your advertising to make an impression. During the opening ceremony of the Atlanta Olympic Games, for example, John Hancock ran a very unusual commercial, one that went on to win numerous awards. Set to the sound of Judy Collins singing "Amazing Grace," the spot told the story of track athletes who won Olympic gold against tremendous odds, including Jesse Owens, Billy Mills, and Wilma Rudolph. The spot was unusual because we were not talking about ourselves; we were focusing on the very thing that makes the Olympic Games great: the courage of the athletes.

When we surveyed consumers after the Games, many of them not only remembered "Amazing Grace" vividly and associated it with the John Hancock brand, but they also assumed that they'd seen it a number of times. Actually, we ran it only once. The truth is, a great ad seen once will have more impact on consumers than a mediocre ad seen 20 times. It's foolish to buy commercial time you don't need.

Finally, don't become fixated on the event itself. The real key to making your sponsorship pay off is to market your association with the sport long before the game and long afterward. We'll talk about how to do that in the next chapter.

THE ATHLETES AND THEIR ENTOURAGES

The third group of players with whom you will probably find yourself negotiating in a sports sponsorship are athletes and their advisors.

Anybody who sponsors the bureaucracy of pro sports without linking his or her brand to the heroics of men and women on the field is probably making a mistake. Reebok, an official licensee and supplier of the 1996 Olympic Games, offers a great lesson in how to waste money by concentrating on the wrong people. I was there in Atlanta for the Games, and I noticed something peculiar about people's feet as I walked around. The officials were all wearing Reebok shoes, but the athletes all seemed to be wearing Nike.

Of course, nobody cared what the officials wore, but everybody cared what American runner Michael Johnson wore when he became the first man in history to win gold medals in both the 200-meter and the 400-meter races. He wore a flashy pair of gold Nikes, which became a central player in the drama of the Games when he gave the shoes to his parents in tribute after his record-breaking performance in the 400. It was a highly emotional moment, pure catnip to broadcasters, who proceeded to spend the next 24 hours blasting closeups of Johnson's gold Nikes into living rooms across the globe. Not surprisingly, surveys after the Games found that a higher percentage of consumers credited nonsponsor Nike with Olympic sponsorship than Reebok.

At John Hancock, we frequently invite world-class athletes to appear at both our business and our charitable events. We try to create as many opportunities as possible for our customers and distributors to meet these athletes. We want people to link our brand with their achievements and to understand that, as a sports sponsor, we help make those achievements possible. But there is one way in which we'd rather not follow the Nike lead: We do not attach our brand too closely to any specific spokesperson.

We simply have no appetite for the risk, though the upside can be huge. In 1998, *Fortune* magazine ran a story called "The Jordan Effect" that credited Michael Jordan with $2.6 billion worth of sales for Nike. *Fortune* theorized that the impact he'd had on the Nike brand was probably worth at least that much again.

The downside, however, can be equally huge, especially if you marry your brand to one of pro sports' seemingly endless supply of tabloid-friendly dunces. Make no mistake, consumers will judge your brand by the company it keeps. Yet, incredibly, brand builders still walk straight into dysfunctional relationships with their eyes open. Converse Shoes, for example, signed Dennis Rodman to a multiyear endorsement deal in 1997, just two weeks after he kicked a courtside photographer in the groin during a Chicago Bulls game. The problem was, after that little performance, what mother in her right mind would buy her son a pair of shoes that made him feel like Dennis Rodman? Needless to say, Converse's All-Star Rodman shoe was not a success.

Nike, of course, has done more to popularize the idea of the athlete as rebel than any other brand. But even Nike, faced with falling sales in the late 1990s and diminishing popularity among teenagers, seems to have had its fill of ugly headlines about Nike-sponsored players. It has actually run a commercial in which a female DJ exhorts athletes, "The drug use, the spousal abuse, the violence—it's got to stop."

My advice is, beware the spokesperson campaign. Even the best-behaved athletes can be problematic if you tie your brand too closely to them. Even if the athlete is personally easy to deal with—and in my experience, many athletes are—they tend to be surrounded by agents and lawyers who justify their existence by solving problems they may well have caused.

I remember once being hung out to dry by the people surrounding the great, and gracious, Joe DiMaggio. He was the long-running and successful spokesperson for a client of our agency, the Bowery Savings Bank. The Bowery had just bought a couple of smaller bank branches in very Italian neighborhoods in New York City and was afraid that there would literally be a run on the bank as soon as they hung out the "under new management" sign.

Somebody at my firm came up with the idea of asking Joe DiMaggio to come to the openings to personally reassure people that there was no reason to move their money—a very good idea. I pulled the short straw and had to call the legend. And he was terrific. He took our offer of a few thousand dollars, and we sent out invitations that said, "Come meet Joe DiMaggio" to the customers of the branches the Bowery had bought.

The responses were incredible, just overwhelming. So I made a call to DiMaggio to confirm his arrangements and let him know how eagerly he was anticipated.

This clearly gave the people representing him a bright idea, because one of them called me a short time later, and said, "Mr. DiMaggio would be happy to come," and then named a figure three times the agreed-upon price. "But you can't do that," I said. "We have a deal."

It turned out they could do it, and did. The officials at the bank naturally blew up at this and, then, in all seriousness, decided that the bank president would be a great replacement for Joe DiMaggio at the branch openings.

My firm gently suggested that we survey a hundred depositors about the switch, giving them a choice between Joe DiMaggio and the bank president. Sure enough, most of them said if DiMaggio didn't show, their money was gone.

So the bank met DiMaggio's fee. I suppose he never knew any of this. He came and charmed all the depositors, and they kept their money with the Bowery. But it could easily have gone the other way, and I've been wary of tying any brand too closely to a single person ever since.

Of course, the good thing about independent sports agents and lawyers like the ones representing Joe DiMaggio—as much as the professional teams and the sponsors tend to complain about them—is that their interests are clear: They represent the athletes and their own pockets.

It's another thing, however, to work with a big sports marketing group, particularly if they want to represent the event as well as the athletes. In that case, the conflicts of interest are likely to make your head spin.

John Hancock had this experience early in our association with the Boston Marathon. Since the BAA wouldn't allow us to pay appearance fees to runners just for showing up for the race, we decided we'd get the world's top runners to Boston another way and give something back to the community at the same time. We'd sponsor running clinics at schools around Massachusetts about the time of the Marathon, and we'd sign the world's best runners to long-term contracts compensating them for conducting those clinics.

Well, a number of the top runners were represented by a big sports marketing firm. And the sports marketing firm refused to let their runners sign our contracts unless we let *them* negotiate the television rights for the Marathon and sell other sponsorships. As far as they were concerned, the athletes were chattel, a bargaining chip they could use to make as much money from the event as possible.

So we did an end run around the sports marketing firm and called the runners directly. "Your agent tells me," I said to them, "that you refuse to run the Boston Marathon because you're not interested in doing clinics for kids." A lot of the runners were very surprised to learn this about themselves, and they wound up defying the agency and coming to Boston anyway.

Here is my advice: If an event is controlled by a sports marketing firm—in other words, if the company is representing not just the athletes, but also the sponsorship rights to the event and the television rights—you should run and not walk away from that event. They simply hold all the cards, and you will be taken advantage of in more ways than you thought possible.

LOOK FOR A BALANCE OF POWER

In the best events, there is a delicate balance of power among the event organizer, the sponsor, the athletes, and the television network. Without that balance, somebody will inevitably kill the goose that lays the golden eggs through overcommercialization or scandal.

The Olympic Games are actually the perfect example of an event in which one player had too much power—the event organizer, the International Olympic Committee. When the IOC's bid city scandal first broke in late 1998, a lot of people outside the Olympic movement were surprised to learn that neither the national Olympic committees nor the individual sports federations, nor the athletes themselves had any vote when it came to the membership of the IOC. It was a completely self-selecting body, and once its members were in, they were in until they were 80 years old, without ever having to stand for reelection. It was also a self-policing body accountable to no government, a highly secretive organization that barred the press from its meetings and failed even to publish an annual report that would allow some public scrutiny of its books. And there was nothing anyone could do about it, since the IOC had exclusive ownership of a very valuable property known as the Olympic Games.

It's not surprising that an organization with so little accountability harbored a degree of corruption, and in 1998 and 1999, the world learned that some of its members were taking gifts from cities hoping to win their bids for the Olympic Games. The really worrisome thing in the wake of these revelations was not the petty form of extortion its individual members had engaged in, but the IOC's failure for many months to enact the structural changes that would keep such a scandal from occuring again.

Fortunately, there were a number of people who refused to allow this self-satisfied club to endanger the most moving and powerful event in the sporting world. So the press and the American government, especially Senator John McCain, kept the IOC's feet to the fire. John Hancock, too, demanded publicly that the IOC remake itself. Although we received a lot of criticism at the time from various members of the Olympic movement for this, I'm proud that John Hancock alone among the top sponsors insisted on structural reforms.

In a special session late in 1999, the IOC did reform, and for an organization steeped in a hundred years of secrecy and self-regard, it reformed to a remarkable degree. It agreed to eliminate its members' visits to bid cities, to require them to regularly stand for reelection, to create financial transparency, and to change the composition of the IOC so that active athletes, national Olympic committees, and international sports federations are all represented on it.

I'm glad that John Hancock played a small part in bringing about those reforms, but I think that the most important thing we accomplished by keeping up the pressure on the IOC is what has been called the "Hancock clause." In 2000, the IOC agreed to an ethics clause in the Olympic sponsorship agreement that allows sponsors to pull out if it ever again engages in any dicey conduct. Now the sponsors, who contribute more than half a billion dollars to the IOC every four years, have half a billion dollars worth of leverage that they didn't have before.

Make sure that when you give the other players in a sponsorship your marketing dollars, you demand some influence in return. Down the road, because of scandal or overcommercialization, you may find yourself having to protect not just your brand, but also the event itself—and you want to have the power to do that.

As a brand builder entering the sponsorship game, you can expect to be wooed by people who live to take advantage of sponsors. These showpeople hope you will be so dazzled by the event or the athletes they control, you won't even notice that they're picking your pocket with one hand, while slapping you on the back with the other.

In other words, the world of corporate sponsorships is not so different from the world of that great American circus impresario P.T. Barnum: You'll find a few genuine wonders and many, many fakes, as well as a lot of sawdust and elephant dung. And Barnum's dictum, "There's a sucker born every minute," applies just as well to the sponsorship world as it did to the big top. Since things move a little faster today, let's change the maxim to read, "There's a sucker born every 30 seconds."

If you want to avoid being one of those suckers, get into the sponsorship game for the right reasons, and be prepared to fight for your interests. Then choose the right property for your brand and manage it aggressively to make sure that it delivers the return on investment P.T. Barnum promised you. That's what we'll talk about next.

6

DO NOT CONFUSE SPONSORSHIP WITH A SPECTATOR SPORT

It's important to remember that all sponsorships are not created equal. And if you intend to use a sponsorship to give your brand a halo, you first have to touch the hearts and minds of consumers. Not every sponsorship will do this for you.

The most coveted and expensive sponsorships, naturally, are those properties that reach many millions of consumers because they draw such huge television audiences, such as the Olympic Games and the NFL. And there is no question that the Olympic Games are absolutely unique, the only sponsorship that both delivers a mass audience and at the same time qualifies as a good cause in consumers' eyes.

The Atlanta Games, for example, were the most watched sporting event in history, with 87 percent of American TV households tuning in at least once. And the Olympics' huge audience is more than ready to give the Games' sponsors a halo: One NBC study found that 85 percent of viewers think of Olympic sponsors as industry leaders, and 80 percent think of them as committed to excellence and quality.

But for other big, televised sporting events, the days are over when you could slap down your money, hang your sign in the stadium, and walk away with the warm wishes of millions of consumers. In one John Hancock survey, for example, we asked consumers about that mother of all American marketing circuses, the Super Bowl. Only 3 out of 10 said they thought better of companies that sponsored the game. In contrast, 8 out of 10 said they thought better of companies that sponsored a benefit for a children's charity.

Unfortunately, pro sports sponsorships leave many consumers cold. There are a lot of problems with those brands called the NBA, the NFL, Major League Baseball, and the NHL, including rising ticket prices, expansion that has diluted the quality of play, overpaid and undersocialized players who generate endless bad press, teams and players too willing to move at the drop of a hat to whatever city is the highest bidder, and the replacement of beloved ballparks with new stadiums full of corporate boxes that push the ordinary fan into the rafters. And the fan response to all of this stuff is well documented. The average ratings for all major televised sports declined 24 percent between 1989 and 1998. For many teams, stadium attendance is down as well. And even those fans who remain loyal to a sport may not appreciate your brand for contributing to the commercial clutter surrounding it.

None of this means, however, that the brand builder should reject pro sports sponsorships outright and forgo their large audiences and broad appeal. It simply takes more care than it once did to make a big-league sports sponsorship pay off for your brand. It's important to keep two things in mind.

First, any brand builder had better choose his or her opportunities carefully. For example, after a prolonged strike and a cancelled World Series in 1994, it looked as if the fans were leaving Major League Baseball never to return, and there seemed to be very little that was positive there for sponsors to use to promote themselves. However, by the late 1990s, John Hancock liked what was happening with the baseball brand. Thanks to Mark McGwire and Sammy Sosa's chase for Roger Maris's home-run record and a general explosion of talent, interest in baseball revived. We thought the sport's classic appeal suited our 140-year-old brand. We liked the fact that the cost per thousand households of advertising on baseball had actually declined since 1994, and we liked the deal we were able to negotiate while baseball was still slumping. So in 2000, we signed on as a major sponsor of Major League Baseball.

The second thing any brand builder had better understand about big-league sports marketing is that it takes hard work to win the goodwill of a jaded audience. You are going to have to make an active effort to connect with consumers and to get them to associate you with all that's best about the sport.

For example, as a baseball sponsor, John Hancock has negotiated the title sponsorship for the All-Star FanFest, a baseball festival that travels with the All-Star Game. Frankly, very few people make it into the All-Star Game itself, except the usual suspects in their corporate boxes, a very limited audience. The John Hancock FanFest, on the other hand, is a much more democratic event. It costs very little to attend, it is open to everybody, it allows the general public to meet some of the game's legendary players, and it expresses more about the pure pleasures of fandom than any other gathering I can think of in the world of pro sports. It also allows us to do something charitable—we give thousands of tickets to underprivileged kids. Yes, John Hancock has its sign in Fenway Park, but the FanFest allows us to reach our potential customers on a more emotional level, and it says more about the empathetic nature of our brand.

In pro sports these days, you have to work hard to achieve a halo effect, but it is achievable.

Conventional sports sponsorships, however, are by no means the only sponsorships that can boost your brand. Philanthropic events, events that combine sports and charity, local events, concerts, ballets, and plays all rank very high in terms of consumers' appreciation for their sponsors. They see these events as good causes. You may reach smaller numbers of people by sponsoring one of them than you would if you signed on with the NFL, but you may affect those people you do reach more deeply, for a fraction of the money.

And don't overlook other opportunities that will allow you to gain a big return on a small investment, such as those offered by emerging sports. When Visa, for example, decided in 1990 to sponsor the decathlon, it was not an obvious choice. The sport was in sorry shape in America. Nonetheless, Visa decided to create an American decathlon team and allow athletes like Dan O'Brien to quit their day jobs. Almost single-handedly, Visa returned this country to the top in the sport, wrapped itself in the flag, linked itself in its customers' minds with some of the bravest athletes in the world, and generated incredible publicity for its brand. All this for about the same price as a single prime-time 30-second television commercial.

Wal-Mart has had similar success with the unlikely sport of bass fishing, managing to lift the profile of the sport at the same time as it has generated new sales with fishing-related promotions. The great advantage of getting involved with an emerging sport like this is that the grateful event organizer is likely to do everything possible to protect the value of your sponsorship. Operation Bass, the company that organizes the fishing tournaments sponsored by Wal-Mart, prohibits the fishermen from wearing the logos of any of its sponsors' competitors when the TV cameras are on. "I'm not going to pay a million dollars in a Wal-Mart parking lot to a guy in a Kmart hat," declared the Operation Bass owner.

Of course, bass fishing is a brilliant choice for Wal-Mart, given the folksy personality of the brand and the company's rural customer base. The general principle here is obvious: A sponsorship, to be effective, should suit your brand. The really astonishing thing, however, is how many corporations sign onto sponsorships seemingly without giving their brands any consideration at all.

NASCAR racing, for example, is an extremely attractive property in many ways. Its audience has grown by leaps and bounds, and NASCAR fans are famously loyal to NASCAR brands. The Cartoon Network, clearly wanting to take advantage of the rising popularity of the sport, sponsors a Winston Cup Series "Wacky Racing" car that has been variously painted with Scooby-Doo, the Powerpuff Girls, and the Flintstones. This cross-promotion, in which the Cartoon Network boosts NASCAR and NASCAR boosts the Cartoon Network, undoubtedly makes economic sense to Turner Broadcasting, which owns the former and broadcasts the latter.

All great on paper. But I wonder what the Cartoon Network is going to do when kids start seeing their favorite cartoon character on the charred and crumpled hood of a car in which the driver died a violent death.

Will it encourage them to love racing or Scooby-Doo? I do not think so.

By the way, we wouldn't put the John Hancock brand on a Winston Cup car, either. We're a life insurer, and we don't particularly want to attach our logo to violent death on the racetrack.

At John Hancock, we get thousands of sponsorship proposals a year and reject a lot of them because they're simply inappropriate for our brand. For example, we once got a call from a promoter asking if we'd be interested in spending $100,000 to help restore the Granary Burying Ground, an historic cemetery in the center of Boston that is the resting place of great patriots such as Samuel Adams, Paul Revere, and our namesake, John Hancock.

We politely told the promoter that we prefer to give our money to the living, not the dead.

He called us again, and again asked us to contribute to the cemetery.

We said, "Sorry, but there's nothing in it for us."

He said, "Yes there is. For $100,000, we'll give you John Hancock."

The idea was that we could exhume the remains and then bury him in front of our headquarters. Once again, we politely declined this fascinating offer.

USE THE SPONSORSHIP EVERY DAY AND IN EVERY WAY

When John Hancock became an Olympic sponsor in 1993, it did more profound things for our brand than we had even hoped. In a certain sense, it gave us an identity.

At the time, we had no companywide marketing program. Instead, we had dozens of people in dozens of departments going off in different directions. One person was doing a program about the heritage and tradition of the company, while another person's program emphasized how modern we were. One person's marketing efforts touted the features of our products, while another person's emphasized the importance of our distributors. The print advertising was naturally very different from the television advertising. Not only were these individual marketing efforts sending out messages that competed with each other, the individual marketing budgets were too tiny to produce very much besides a lot of incremental waste. This lack of coherence in marketing is, by the way, an incredibly common problem in American business.

Then, in 1993, we signed on as a worldwide sponsor of the Olympic Games, and, for the first time, we were able to convince our individual department managers to design their marketing materials around a single theme. Yes, there was some grousing from the people we were boxing in, but less than you might think. This is America, after all, and Americans love to rally around sports.

Suddenly, we were able to get tremendous leverage out of our spending. A lot of small marketing budgets that used to be spent on efforts that cancelled each other out were now behaving like one big marketing budget spent in a very focused and disciplined manner.

The advantages for our brand were enormous. For the first time, there was a discernible consistency and style in all our communications, and it was easier for consumers to figure out who we were. Since our Olympic sponsorship happens to come with the right to use the single, most readily recognized symbol on the planet, the five interlocking rings, John Hancock uses the Olympic rings on everything we produce: our letterhead, business cards, sales materials, and annual reports, as well as the tag for our television commercials. We have even used the rings on our signs at Red Sox and Celtics games. The International Olympic Committee initially objected to our use of their logo in non-Olympic sporting venues, fearing people would confuse the Celtics games with an Olympic event, but I pointed out that they had a more discerning viewership than they thought. Anyone could tell by the quality of the basketball (good) that it wasn't the Olympic Games.

The Olympic rings help John Hancock reinforce certain essential things about our brand over and over, in every line of business and in every market: that we are willing to support something our customers consider a good cause and that we are a big player. In truth, the rings suggest that we are a much bigger player than we actually are, given the company they put us in. The 10 other top Olympic sponsors include corporations like Coca-Cola and McDonald's, whose market capitalization dwarfs ours.

However, the Olympic Games offer us much more than just a logo. They offer us a platform for all our marketing efforts. We use the two weeks of the Games themselves to entertain our best clients and distributors and to reward our best employees and sales representatives.

We've also sponsored tours of both figure skating and gymnastics champions that enable us to bring our Olympic sponsorship to life in dozens of American cities even in the off years. Events surrounding these Hancock tours allow our salespeople to reach out to thousands of potential customers by inviting them to come meet an Olympic athlete or to bring their gymnastics-crazy daughters to a clinic run by legendary coach Bela Karolyi. There is tremendous romance to this kind of grassroots marketing. If you'd like to create the biggest possible halo for your brand, few things beat giving someone who never expected to have a brush with athletic greatness the chance to experience it firsthand.

A really good sponsorship like the Olympic Games or Major League Baseball has such broad appeal that we are able to use it for every line of business we're in and with every audience that matters to us: consumers, large institutional clients, distributors of all kinds, and our own employees (95 percent of whom have attended some Olympic-connected event, and a number of whom have told me that they think our association with the Olympics gives them something to live up to).

Amortizing a sponsorship over all your marketing activities is not only good for your brand, but also probably the only way to justify the cost. The truth is, many sponsorship opportunities are extremely expensive. For example, to sign on as an Olympic partner, from 2001–2004, you could expect to pay the IOC some $65 million. It might cost you that much again just to buy advertising time on the Olympic broadcasts. And yet there is so much commercial noise during the Games that if you take surveys immediately after them, consumers are just as likely to assume your competitors were sponsors as you.

If you expect to just come into an event, plunk down your millions, run your commercials, and then leave, your sponsorship will have all the longevity of a potato chip in a fire. The key to getting consumers to make the connection between your sponsorship and your brand is to market it in every way and all the time, during the off-season as well as on.

And constantly promoting a sponsorship is the only way to take the sting out of one of the great frustrations of event marketing: being ambushed by a competitor who hasn't paid the sponsorship fees, but is able to convince consumers that it has.

Wendy's, for example, has regularly ambushed official sponsor McDonald's at the Olympic Games, most notoriously at Lillehammer in 1994, when it bought $8 million worth of commercial time on the Games broadcast in order to run a series of Olympic-themed commercials featuring Dave Thomas. I'm sure those commercials confused a few people as to which company was really the official Olympic burger brand, but ultimately, Wendy's hasn't been able to steal the value of McDonald's sponsorship because McDonald's is a very energetic Olympic sponsor. Through charitable ventures surrounding the Games, promotions in its restaurants, and Olympic programs for its employees, McDonald's links its brand with the Olympic rings in consumers' minds long before the Games begin and long after they are over.

SET THE RIGHT EXPECTATIONS

Clearly, I believe in actively managing a sponsorship. Many sponsors, however, are essentially passive, content to simply hang their logo in a stadium, vaguely hoping this newfound fame will translate into sales, and to leave it at that. They may pay lip service to the "halo effect," and tell you that they bought into an event in order to touch the hearts and minds of consumers, but they aim way too low in practice, going after little more than name recognition.

Of course, name recognition may be one of your goals for your sponsorship, particularly if you're a relatively unknown brand. And hanging your logo courtside may be smart, because it can mean the TV cameras are constantly on you, and you're getting huge advertising equivalencies.

But the further out from the court you get, away from the TV cameras, the worse an investment signage becomes. The marketers who buy the tunnel-portals at football stadiums at hundreds of thousands of dollars a pop are amazing to me. A large portion of the fans who see them are season ticket holders to begin with, the same people for all eight home games. And a large percentage of *them* have been drinking all day at tailgate parties and can't read your sign anyway. You wind up paying a fortune for every sober read.

The worst investment of all is putting your name on the building. I know, a lot of corporations pay millions to name sports facilities after themselves, and pro sports is now full of such romantic-sounding destinations as Enron Field. My advice is, beware the edifice complex.

In one survey John Hancock commissioned, we found that only 15 percent of consumers said that naming a stadium after your company would make them more likely to purchase your products. But more than twice as many people said that they are actively *hostile* to a company that changes the name of a facility to its own name. And I bet we could have doubled their hostility if we'd reminded them of the overpriced nachos with plastic cheese that those stadiums are serving—or, how badly the home team is playing.

You may get name recognition out of a stadium deal, but your name is likely to be mud.

If many sponsors aim too low, there are also a few that aim too high. IBM, for example, decided to use the Atlanta Olympic Games as a chance to show off its technology to the world, creating the largest temporary computer network in human history as the official technology supplier. You have to give IBM credit for courage.

However, it couldn't quite live up to its promises. Glitches appeared in the very worst of all possible places: the IBM system that was supposed to deliver instant information to international newswire services, which would then disseminate it to the world. And, unfortunately, those glitches had an air of absurdity that reporters found irresistible. One boxer was described as being 2 feet tall; another was 21 feet tall. The system failed to yield results for contests that had taken place, but claimed that a Dane and an Australian set new world records in a bicycle race that hadn't yet occurred.

Eventually, IBM was reduced to faxing the results to the media center and running them to the news agencies. High tech had become humiliatingly low tech. And for the estimated $80 million it spent in Atlanta, IBM got little except a beating in the world press that made every marketer in America wince in sympathy.

Fortunately, IBM redeemed itself with its performance in Nagano, but the lesson is clear: The risks associated with in-kind marketing are huge. A value-in-kind sponsorship puts your products on stage in front of the world. If you deliver anything less than perfection, you can injure your brand.

MAKE SURE YOU ACHIEVE SOMETHING MEASURABLE AND REAL

Most brand builders start out in event marketing as wide-eyed innocents. They get in without any clear way of determining what they're getting out of the deal. An example that leaps immediately to mind is a big technology brand that spent $4 million in 1997 sponsoring its second college bowl game.

When a *New York Times* reporter asked the company's marketing director after the game how he knew he'd gotten his money's worth, the marketing director admitted his company had no empirical way to measure the value of the sponsorship. "But ask yourself," the marketing director said, "is there a value associated with showing people a good time?"

There is for one kind of event. I believe it's called *dating*.

But if all you are doing as a sponsor is showing people a good time, you are wasting your money. Sponsorships are investments—often, big investments—and you should expect a concrete return from them. That return can take many forms:

- You can create so much good publicity that the advertising equivalencies cover the sponsorship fees.

- You can experience such a rise in public esteem for your brand that that alone may make the event worthwhile.

- You can generate enough sales to justify the investment by using the event to introduce yourself to consumers and gather leads.

- You can also boost sales by using an event as a promotion, by entertaining clients at the event, or by using the event as a reward for your salespeople.

- You may even find the sponsorship worthwhile simply for the things it does to enhance your relationship with the people who matter most to the business, both internally and externally.

A sponsorship can pay for itself in one or all of these ways, but be sure that it does pay for itself. At John Hancock, we not only spend time and money promoting our sponsorships, we spend time and money measuring their impact. We believe that if you can't prove that a given sponsorship is working for your brand, it probably isn't, and you should probably get out.

Event marketing is not a gentle game. The rules are tough: Choose only those properties that add luster to your brand, negotiate aggressively to protect the value of the sponsorship, use it to create a consistent marketing platform, use it in the off-season, make sure it gives you a real return, and say sayonara if it doesn't.

Don't allow the circuslike atmosphere that surrounds most sponsorships to fool you into thinking that they are a day at the circus. They are first and foremost a business proposition, and the more they are treated that way, the better an investment they will prove for the long-term success of your brand.

7

DO NOT ALLOW SCANDAL TO DESTROY IN 30 DAYS A BRAND THAT TOOK 100 YEARS TO BUILD

If the two most certain things in life are death and taxes, the two most certain things in business are competition and scandal. Bad press threatens every business at some time or other. The fact that scandal is so common and so inevitable, however, doesn't mean it isn't also ferociously damaging to your brand if you fail to prepare for it or if you handle it badly when it does occur.

For example, no one over a certain age will ever hear the name "Exxon" again without thinking, *"Exxon Valdez* disaster," and remembering the company's apparently indifferent response to the news that millions of gallons of Exxon oil were befouling the Alaskan coastline after a tanker ran aground. And Perrier, which once had a 45 percent share of America's imported mineral water market, has still not recovered from the discovery of trace amounts of benzene in its water in 1990. The health threat was reportedly minimal, but the lingering suspicion of the brand was not.

Brands are like Fabergé eggs. It takes incredible skill to create them, but only one clumsy move to destroy them. Handling scandal is therefore one of the most delicate and important jobs of any brand builder.

The first rule is that it is much less painful to inoculate your company against scandal in good times than it is to try to find a cure during an onslaught of bad publicity.

BRAND IS DESTINY

Consider for a moment the popularity of the Gulf War. Sure, there were substantive reasons that we Americans proved so ready, willing, and able to consider Saddam Hussein a threat to our national interest. But I've often thought there was another contributing factor: The guy just had such a bad brand. There was that Hitler-esque moustache. There was that obnoxious vanity, with Saddam portraits plastered all over Baghdad. And most significant, there was that name, which sounds like a cross between "sodomy" and "Goddammit!" Would we have bombed Iraq if it had been headed by a guy named Winston? Maybe not.

Your brand is your fate. Its character determines how any piece of negative information will affect you. The same scandal that might cripple one brand will only graze another.

It is therefore crucial to persuade people to think well of your company before you really need them to. There are a million ways to do this, ranging from building good products and allowing civil return policies to sponsoring worthy events and engaging in corporate philanthropy. John Hancock, for example, has garnered reams of good press for saving the Boston Marathon and for philanthropic efforts such as our "Summer of Opportunity" program that gives at-risk kids internships in our offices. And the benign image we've created for our brand with everything from our Olympic sponsorship to our television commercials has helped us survive a serious scandal I'll talk about later in the chapter.

If you fail to create a worthy image for your brand, by the time you need to look like something other than a greedy maniac, it's generally too late to do anything about it.

However genuine his intentions, junk bond king Mike Milken's increasing interest in philanthropy as the government circled in on him for insider trading was derided in the press as a transparent public relations ploy. And it's unfortunate for Microsoft that Bill Gates didn't start giving away the billions he gave away in 1999 a few years earlier, before the Justice Department's antitrust case against the company grew so serious. If he'd appeared to be a great philanthropist a little sooner, it might not have changed the legal outcome, but it might have softened the rapacious image of the Microsoft brand and made the legal judgment against the company less damning in the eyes of its customers, competitors, employees, and distributors.

If you have done the right thing and built up sufficient goodwill through your brand-building efforts in good times, when scandal comes—and it will come—you at least have some insulation. Consumers, stockholders, and all those people who make a living being critical of corporations—Wall Street analysts, the press, regulators, etc.—may criticize you, but they will at least give you an opportunity to correct the situation.

That's because people's relationship with a brand is like a relationship with a spouse. If there is a foundation of trust and respect, the relationship is likely to survive a single indiscretion. And that's important, because smart companies rarely make the same mistake twice. "Oh, my dear," you can then say, "I've lied to you, but give me a chance and I'll never do it again." You might, *might* get that chance.

On the other hand, if there's been suspicion all along—or even just coldness and neglect—the same indiscretion may be unforgivable. It doesn't matter how loudly you repent. "Here's your suitcase," consumers will say. Your brand is out.

Probably the greatest example in modern times of a well-insulated brand is Bill Clinton. For all the hoopla surrounding the Monica Lewinsky case, with the public, at least, the Clinton brand was ultimately protected from the scandal; and it was his Republican enemies who wound up hurting their brands during his impeachment trial. The truth is, whatever Clinton's faults, most Americans approved of his job performance as president. They'd already decided they pretty much liked the Clinton brand. And since this brand was never about chaste behavior in the first place—in 1992, before we had even elected him, Clinton as much as admitted on *60 Minutes* that he'd cheated on his wife—a sex scandal was not going to undo the goodwill engendered by budget surpluses, a raging economy, and welfare reform.

In other words, Clinton had built up enough chits to be forgiven for looking like a horse's ass. Every brand builder should take lessons from this man—well, *some* lessons.

DO NOT ALLOW YOUR ENEMIES TO DEFINE YOU

Of course, I'd like to think one of the reasons Clinton handled scandal so well is that he went to school on Michael Dukakis's 1988 presidential campaign. I was Dukakis's advertising director during the last months of this debacle; and while Clinton's people were smart enough in 1992 to figure out what mistakes not to repeat, I made a point of imparting as many of the painful lessons I'd learned as I could.

The 1988 campaign was primarily a branding campaign, with both sides launching competing new brands at the same time. It didn't matter that George Bush had been vice president for almost eight years and that President Reagan had given him many assignments. The polling still indicated that most people thought the vice president's job involved nothing more than going to funerals and waiting for the president to die. In the public's mind, Bush was still undefined, and so was Governor Dukakis, who was new to the national stage.

The rule in marketing is that there are only three ways you can define yourself: You can be better, you can be cheaper, or you can attack. Politics is much the same, except that you have only months, not years, to define your brand.

In 1988, the Bush campaign decided that the way to win was to attack, and they were very clever about how they did it. They didn't begin with an all-out national campaign. Instead, they started regionally, in Texas, with some commercials about Dukakis's position on gun control. Then, in various spots throughout the country, Bush supporters started spreading information about Willie Horton, the convicted murderer who beat and stabbed a man and raped his fiancée while out on a furlough from a Massachusetts prison during the Dukakis administration. And when these first attacks went unchecked, Bush's supporters kept spreading them quietly underneath the radar of the media-monitoring services we had at the time.

When the attacks finally registered with the Dukakis campaign in the summer of 1988, the "powers that be" decided they were not meaningful. They were too sporadic. They seemed to come and go, show up and then disappear. And because the attacks were so incendiary and ugly, and contained an element of racism in their exploitation of white fears about minority crime, the campaign thought they wouldn't be taken seriously.

It was a fundraiser from Texas—a huge guy, a former Texas Ranger—who first made it clear to me just how stupid the campaign's position was. It was a Sunday afternoon, and we were talking about moving Dukakis's definition along in Texas. And he said, "You all don't understand. Sure, not everybody believes George Bush is a Texan. The trouble is, *everybody* believes this small, short, dark Greek Dukakis wants to become president of the United States in order to take away our guns and allow our women to be raped. So to that extent, his policy on saving the redwoods ain't exactly important to us in Texas."

This guy instinctively understood one of the key rules of marketing: do not allow your enemy to define you. Because if you allow yourself to be defined negatively, nothing positive you say about yourself will register. In other words, no one cares how sensitive you are on the subject of sequoias if they already believe you're the best friend a criminal could ever have.

The great fallacy about the Dukakis campaign is that he lost the election because his failure to answer the other camp's attacks made him look weak. But the real story was more complicated. It wasn't that the attacks made him seem less macho. Instead, they made him into something to be actively feared. It was a definition problem. We'd failed to define him positively and failed to deflect the negative definition provided by Bush's supporters, so that negative definition stuck. Once that happens, it takes five times the effort and money to redefine yourself positively. Ten million dollars' worth of advertising in the last weeks of the campaign and the right message—that Dukakis, unlike that elitist George Bush, was "on your side"—gave Dukakis a boost, but not enough to push us out of the hole we had allowed the Bush camp to dig for us.

Bill Clinton and his people were not about to let this happen to them, which is why his campaign set up its famous "rapid response" team that was ready to refute any attack by the next news cycle. Campaign strategist James Carville put it this way: "The first law is that the public cannot react to information that they don't have. If all they hear is one thing, you can't expect them to know something else if you don't tell them."

In other words, it takes a certain humility to outwit bad press. This is as true in business as it is in politics. You may know yourself to be above reproach, but the public won't know unless you tell them. You may know an accusation to be scurrilous and false, or true but irrelevant, or so silly it's not even worth your contempt—but again, the public won't know unless you tell them. Any time scandal looms, it's important to swallow your pride and explain yourself. Yet, over and over, companies take the Dukakis campaign's approach, ruining their brands with an arrogant refusal to answer the charges against them.

Thanks to the high-handed way it handled public fears about both the health and environmental consequences of genetically modified food crops in the late 1990s, Monsanto, for example, allowed environmental activists to turn it into the archenemy of nature—the butterfly-killing, Frankenfood-making "Monsatan." Obviously, I am not equipped to judge the science of genetically modified foods, but I am equipped to judge the public relations, and they have not been very smart. Monsanto lobbied ferociously against labels for genetically modified food products. It even threatened to sue dairies that labeled their products free of the gene-altered bovine growth hormone it produces. The argument was that such labeling makes safe products seem sinister.

Of course, what *really* seems sinister is the refusal to give intelligent consumers the information they need to make a choice. Many of today's consumers grew up on *Life Magazine* pictures of thalidomide babies. They are not about to be convinced that it's safe to ingest something as unnatural as soybeans whose DNA has been altered so the plants tolerate spraying with weed killer, just because the company that stands to make millions from the soybean seed says, "Trust us. It's safe."

Instead of creating an atmosphere of trust, Monsanto created an environment that suggested there was something to hide.

Not surprisingly, Monsanto's attempt to control the flow of information backfired. The European market refused to go near genetically modified crops. American farmers started shying away from planting the modified crops because they couldn't sell them abroad and because giant domestic customers such as H.J. Heinz, Gerber, and Frito-Lay no longer wanted them in their products. And legislation was introduced in congress in early 2000 to require food labeling.

As the CEO of DuPont, another large manufacturer of genetically engineered seed, said in a speech in 1998, "Public concern has been aggravated by the perception that we in the biotech industry have often acted as though public fears are not legitimate and are the result of ignorance." Exactly.

And even when public fears *are* the result of ignorance, that is still no excuse for ignoring them. In 1993, an elderly couple claimed they found a syringe in a can of Diet Pepsi, and dozens of copycat claims followed. Pepsi, to its credit, took the charges very seriously; and in a particularly effective bit of crisis management, took the terror out of the situation by releasing videos that showed how the high-speed canning process inside a Pepsi plant is designed specifically to prevent contamination. The tape was picked up by news organizations all over the country. The contamination scare was quickly dismissed as a hoax, a number of pathetic attention seekers were arrested for making the false claims, and there were no lingering effects for the Pepsi brand.

The advent of the Internet, of course, means that negative stories about your brand don't even have to pass the not-so-stringent smell test of the traditional media before reaching thousands, even millions of people. In 1999, Procter & Gamble's Febreze fabric deodorizer was the victim of the Internet-bred rumor that it killed pets. This was pure misinformation—there was not a single shred of evidence that anything in the product was harmful to animals. Nonetheless, the company created a website to debunk the story, enlisted the help of the Humane Society and the American Society for the Prevention of Cruelty to Animals to point out its inaccuracy, and made the safety of the product clear on its packaging. It's a good thing Procter & Gamble was not too proud to address the question, because competitors Resolve and Clorox FreshCare both seemed willing to take advantage of the rumor, offering coupons that pronounced their products safe for pets.

The truth is, these corporate rumors seem to have a life of their own, and all of us have heard them—that Mountain Dew reduces sperm counts, that worms have been found in McDonald's hamburgers, that the Coors company supports the Nazi party. Professor Gary Alan Fine, the author of the book *Manufacturing Tales: Sex and Money in Contemporary Legends,* has documented something he calls "The Goliath Effect": These rumors are far more likely to be attached to the largest or most prestigious corporations in an industry.

119

Discussing a number of rumors that have attached themselves to McDonald's, Professor Fine points out, "This large collection of stories is striking in contrast to the paucity of tales about Burger King, the second-largest hamburger chain. . . . The corporate dominance of McDonald's preempts legends about other establishments."[1]

In other words, the bigger your brand, the more likely you are to attract a negative story, truth being irrelevant to the question. According to Professor Fine, these corporate legends flourish because, as a society, we need them. "We can't talk about our fear of large corporations," he told a reporter with the *Orlando Sentinel* in 1993, "the fear that they may be poisoning us. It makes us sound paranoid. But we can say, 'Kentucky Fried Chicken put a rat in the batter!'"

Today's consumers grew up on Watergate, DDT, Three Mile Island, and the *Exxon Valdez* disaster. They are inherently suspicious of big institutions, and no brand builder should ever forget it. A big brand is therefore a double-edged sword. Popularity can help you survive a scandal, but it can also make you a lightning rod for scandal.

It's the king-of-the-mountain problem. It's always fascinating to watch the guy on top fall. And a kind of media rubbernecking always follows.

This means only one thing: If you're a high-flying brand and something negative comes at you, it's dangerous not to handle it. If the charge is crazy, prove it—but don't think that its craziness alone will make it powerless to hurt you. Look at poor Mike

---

[1] Gary Alan Fine, *Manufacturing Tales: Sex and Money in Contemporary Legends* (Knoxville: The University of Tennessee Press, 1992) p. 147.

Dukakis. He was not about to set the country's murderers and rapists free, but they never knew that in Texas.

DO NOT STALL. DO NOT ALLOW THE LAWYERS TO STALL

For every scandal that works like the 1971 Bon Vivant soup scandal, where a banker dies of botulism one day, and the company files for bankruptcy three weeks later, there are a thousand that fester over the course of years.

Sure, a few customer complaints roll in about your products, or a few bad stories appear in the news about the labor practices in your factories or discrimination in your offices, and maybe you get sued a few times and settle quietly—and all the while you think the problem has been contained. Denial is as powerful a force in business as it is in life. But scandal often operates like an insidious poison that seeps gradually into the public consciousness. It's a process of gradual disenfranchisement, as more and more consumers and more and more distributors start to associate you with something negative.

You may not even understand why you've become second tier, why you're selling in the bargain basement stores now and not the top stores, or why your products are dramatically discounted. Or you may understand it, but still think you'll take your chances, given the incredible cost of acknowledging a problem. It could cost hundreds of millions of dollars to voluntarily recall your products or to admit the kind of fault that requires a legal remedy. Maybe you're afraid to take the financial hit, afraid to say anything publicly. Maybe the financial people and lawyers inside the company are winning the debate, those people who say respectively, "Spend nothing" and "Acknowledge nothing."

What generally happens, however, if you don't correct the situation, is that there will be more and more incidents. Then suddenly, the tipping point is reached, you're on the front page of the *New York Times* looking like Snidely Whiplash, a government agency is ordering you to make amends, and your stock and your sales are plummeting like rocks. And you find you've protected your earnings for a few quarters at the cost of ruining your brand.

The truth is, a good brand will protect a stupid company in a time of scandal, but it will not protect an irresponsible company. Consumers and investors will forgive you if you make a mistake and own up to it. But they will punish you badly for withholding, covering up, or stalling.

The Perrier case I mentioned earlier offers a great example of a brand permanently damaged by a lack of candor on the part of management. When scientists in North Carolina found traces of benzene—a known carcinogen—in Perrier water in early 1990, Perrier initially insisted the problem was isolated to certain bottling lines for North America. Wishful thinking, clearly, given the cost of a larger recall. The company even minimized the problem to the point that it blamed a single benzene-soaked rag—even though, as the *Washington Post* reported, company officials already knew that the problem was considerably bigger. The filters that routinely removed the naturally occurring benzene in the water had not been replaced as they should have been, and they had tainted all of the company's output, not just the stuff intended for America. When laboratory tests in several European countries found benzene in the Perrier there, Perrier was an object of outrage for attempting to pull the wool over its European customers' eyes. It instituted a worldwide recall, but the brand never recovered from the perception that it was unsafe. Competitors moved in and carved up Perrier's market share; and in early 2000, the brand's revenue was still 40 percent smaller than it was in 1989.

The Perrier story is now textbook, but incredibly, there are still companies that haven't done the reading assignment. When the Firestone tire scandal broke in 2000 with the revelation that in hot weather, the treads on certain Firestone tires, made largely for Ford Explorers, would separate, there were two particularly damning pieces of information for the Firestone brand: First, Ford's claim that Firestone had begun receiving complaints about its tires as early as 1997; and second, the revelation that there had been more than 100 deaths before Firestone finally initiated a recall. Whether Firestone was slow to react as the result of a deliberate decision not to admit fault or because the company had not put adequate systems in place to monitor the safety of its products doesn't really matter. Either way, the company failed to protect its end-users.

In a case like this, it's not just a faulty tire model that seems dangerous, but the callous attitudes of an entire company. In the days after Firestone instituted the recall, one tire store owner told the *Wall Street Journal*: "We had one lady who bought top-of-the-line Firestone tires a month ago come in, and she just wants them off." It did not matter that hers were not the problem tires. She no longer trusted the brand.

If you make consumers suspect that you'd sacrifice their well-being for your bottom line, your brand is finished. Therefore, if there is even a chance that consumers will personalize any negative information about your brand—in other words, think, "Oh, my gosh, the person that brand failed to protect could have been *me*"—it is time to step forward and act responsibly.

The really smart brands, of course, smell a potential scandal long before it explodes and get out in front of it. For example, De Beers, the South African-controlled company that sells two-thirds of the world's uncut diamonds, sensed a potential consumer backlash brewing because of so-called "blood diamonds" that were financing ugly civil wars in Angola, Sierra Leone, and the Congo.

Instead of waiting until protestors were smashing engagement rings everywhere its name appeared, De Beers took control and decided it would not do business with anyone who trafficked in these diamonds. In 2000, De Beers announced that its selling arm would put a written guarantee on every invoice that the stones do not come from areas of Africa controlled by rebel forces. De Beers also introduced a new logo it called the "forevermark" to distinguish its politically correct stones from those of more dubious origin. In one swoop, it managed to appear socially responsible and increase the cachet of its diamonds.

The truth is, a scandal handled quickly and responsibly enough can actually enhance your brand's stature. The classic example of this is Tylenol. Conventional wisdom in 1982 was that the brand would never recover after seven deaths were traced to cyanide inserted into Extra-Strength Tylenol capsules. But parent company Johnson & Johnson's rapid response said very clearly that this brand put consumers first. The company actually told consumers not to use its products until the tampering was investigated. Though the deaths all occurred in the Chicago area, Johnson & Johnson instituted a national recall of all Tylenol capsules. It stopped advertising and making the capsules before returning to the market with a tamper-proof packaging.

The recall cost $100 million in the short term, but it was the best of all possible moves in the long term, both for Tylenol customers and Johnson & Johnson shareholders. The brand is so trusted today that Tylenol products retain a dominant 25 percent share of the internal analgesics market.

YOU CAN RUN—BUT YOU CANNOT HIDE

John Hancock has watched one particular scandal unfold with a rather personal interest—the life insurance industry's sales practices scandal of the mid-1990s. Certain insurance agents were found to be "churning," convincing people who owned life insurance policies with accumulated cash value to use them to fund new larger policies. Frequently, the customers were not aware that their cash value was being drained to buy these new policies, or they were told inaccurately that policy dividends would soon cover the premiums. And the primary purpose of these sales was to generate commissions for the agents.

When John Hancock discovered in the early 1990s that some of our agents were engaging in these deceptive sales practices, we did the sensible thing. We terminated them. In 1992, ahead of many of our competitors, we put a corrective mechanism in place: an ethics review board independent of our sales operation, which established clear ethical standards for our salespeople and reviewed questionable cases. The next year, we expanded this effort into a sales practices unit that reviewed agent-created sales materials and trained agents in ethical selling. We changed our commission structure to discourage these problematic policy replacement sales. And in 1995, when we were the subject of a class-action lawsuit over the deceptive sales practices of the past, we settled. Some of our salespeople had done the wrong thing, and we acknowledged it, so the damage to our brand was minimal.

One of our competitors, however, was not so lucky. By its own admission, it failed to clamp down decisively enough on unethical life insurance sales practices in the early 1990s. Then, when regulators began examining those sales practices and policyholders filed suit, it inflamed the scandal by appearing to fight the charges on every front.

This is a classic mistake in a scandal. You know you're wrong, but you think somehow you can hide from the consequences of your misdeed if you just don't admit too much. Meanwhile, the law grinds slowly away at you, the regulators grind slowly away, and the media grinds slowly away, and your brand grows more and more negative in consumers' eyes. In the end, you discover that you can run but you cannot hide. And you've done little by fighting except keep the scandal alive for years; when, if you'd owned up to your faults and taken your medicine, the problem might have quickly disappeared.

Our competitor made one other classic mistake in attempting to battle its sales practices scandal: It launched an enormous advertising campaign in the middle of it, talking about its trustworthiness as newspaper headlines were proclaiming the opposite. In other words, the brand turned to poison temporarily; so what they decided to do was feed people even more of it. Well, there is a huge difference in credibility between the things editors and reporters say about you and the things you say about yourself. And if you try to advertise your way out of a scandal, you may do little more than remind consumers why they dislike you. After its tire scandal broke in 2000, Firestone at least had the good sense to downplay a planned 100th anniversary celebration.

Our competitor appeared not to understand that its brand was at stake in all this, but it was. Between 1994 and 1999, during the greatest economic boom in history, the amount of life insurance this company issued fell by 35 percent. During the same period, the amount of life insurance issued by John Hancock rose by almost the same amount; and in 1999, we wound up on the *New York Times'* list of the 100 best brands of the century. The difference was, John Hancock was able to convince consumers that we cared that people had been cheated. Whatever its intentions, this other company was apparently not able to do the same thing.

The truly cruel thing about a badly handled scandal is that people may not give you credit for the good things you do going forward. Years after most consumers have forgotten the facts of the case, they may still look at your brand on the shelves and feel that something is vaguely distasteful there.

Your brand may be enveloped in an air of mistrust for decades. It may never recover.

It can take 100 years to build a good brand and 30 days of bad publicity to destroy it. Don't allow this to happen to you. Do all you can to inoculate your brand against scandal. Then treat every scandal that does appear as an opportunity to demonstrate the extreme integrity of your brand.

When you're wrong, admit it and make amends. When you're not, prove it and move on.

8

MAKE YOUR DISTRIBUTORS SLAVES TO YOUR BRAND

It's amazing, actually, to consider how little power American consumers have had over the years, compared with the people who have distributed goods and services to them. Sure, American consumers have always benefited from the national gift for entrepreneurship, but they have also always been subject to the tyranny of the geography. This is a very big country. Before consumers could buy anything, somebody had to be willing to sell it in their corner of the world.

One hundred and thirty years ago, this meant that unless you lived in a big city, you probably shopped at a general store. If it was winter and you needed a coat, and the general store had *any* coat in *any* size, regardless of weight or quality or price, you would probably buy it—or trade a sheep for it—and be grateful.

Then the Montgomery Ward and Sears, Roebuck catalogs arrived at the end of the 19th century, and they were a tremendous improvement. Even if you lived in a town as remote as say, Tucson, you would now have a choice of sizes and styles. Of course, you might have to order your jacket the previous spring to get it before winter; but still, you were grateful even for the chance to buy it.

Then came the department stores that started blanketing the country to serve consumers who now had cars to bring them to the shops. The department stores offered a smattering of everything, but a limited choice in any one thing. Still, you were unlikely even to know what you were missing out on. You bought what they stocked and were grateful.

Then came the category-killer superstores. They had every major brand of whatever it was you wanted under one roof. Of course, they also had boxes stacked to the ceiling, aisles that stretched on into eternity, and sales help that tended to be both scarce and uninformed. Still, if they actually had what you wanted in stock, you put up with the shopping experience, and were grateful. At the same time, there were also increasing opportunities to shop by mail. This was convenient, but essentially hit or miss. If you happened to be on the right mailing list and the right catalog with the right jacket showed up just as the days were getting chilly, well, you ordered it and were grateful.

Then, of course, came the Internet and the absolute end of unearned gratitude.

THE INTERNET AND THE LIBERATED CONSUMER

Type almost anything you are looking for into an online search engine, and you have your choice of a dozen distributors. Geography is no longer a barrier. You can order from a store 10 states or 10 countries away, and it's just as convenient as strolling down the street to a store in the neighborhood. You can choose whether to buy from the upscale specialist that carries only the finest and rarest items, or the big warehouse that has only the most common things but offers the best price on them, or another variety of distributor somewhere in between. And the smartest of these online distributors understands something that has eluded many bricks-and-mortar businesses: For busy people with a lot of choices, the quality of the shopping experience will make or break a brand.

In the case of Amazon.com, cracker-jack distribution *is* the brand. Amazon certainly did not turn the book business on its head by offering consumers the same pleasures as a really good independent bookstore. There is nothing impressive about Amazon's "personal" recommendations, the descriptions of the books it sells, or its editorial judgments. No, Amazon has succeeded because it is utterly superior as a distributor; and to customers who know what they want, that is what counts. The experience of shopping Amazon—the tremendous selection, the willingness to track down out-of-print books, the one-click ordering that adds new meaning to the phrase "impulse buying," the quick delivery—is all about the joys of a friction-free distribution system. You get precisely what you want with a minimum of effort.

And the management of Amazon.com are intelligent enough to understand that this ease of use is what sets the brand apart, which is why the company sued to keep competitors from copying its one-click order technology. It's also why, during the fateful Christmas of 1999, when a number of e-commerce sites were unable to deliver on their promises, Amazon overspent on inventory and order fulfillment in order to make sure it did not disappoint any of its customers. It may have lost money in the short term, but it protected its brand in the long term.

Of course, the story of retailing over the Internet thus far has been all about the struggle for profitability, and many online stores have already come and gone. But any old-world brand builder who takes comfort from these shakeouts and thinks he or she won't have to compete with lightning-quick Internet companies or make his or her distribution consumer-friendly is engaging in fantasy. Consumers have shopped Amazon.com now, and there is no way you're ever going to get them back on the farm.

DEATH OF THE SALESMEN

Distributors used to have as much power over the brands they sold as they did over consumers. Whether the distributor was a toy store, an insurance agency, a car dealership, or a supermarket, the principle was the same. They were the gatekeepers. And unless a brand was so powerful in consumers' minds that they walked into the distributor, banged on the counter, and said,

"Why aren't you selling this product?," the distributors held all the cards.

They could determine the fate of your brand simply by deciding to stick you on a low shelf or in a dark corner. They were in a position to negotiate a huge cut of every item they sold, reducing your margins to nothing. They might decide to carry you, but not in a volume sufficient to justify your overhead. They might say, "If the stuff sells well, we'll give you a big order." That's not much of a commitment. But you had better borrow the money to keep the factory lights lit and the assembly line moving. Because if you happened to get lucky and your brand took off, and you didn't have more inventory to push into their markets right away, your distributors would *destroy* you.

Of course, it was to the distributors' advantage to have as much exclusivity as possible over the brands they sold, and they often consolidated their power by convincing manufacturers to distribute their way or no way.

This is how entire industries wound up moving their products in ways that consumers manifestly hate. The classic example, of course, is the automobile industry. Until the advent of online car-shopping sites like Autobytel.com and CarsDirect.com, car dealers were able to force almost every consumer—including the majority of them who find haggling distasteful—to haggle over price. They forced consumers to do this negotiation without an essential piece of information, the dealer cost. And they forced them to collect information about their cars from a salesperson who was rewarded for selling them anything, whether it was what the consumer needed or not.

People are so angry about having to buy this way, that in 1999, J.D. Power and Associates characterized 33 percent of new car buyers—the biggest and youngest group—as "armed unfriendlies." They're armed with the dealer's cost they got off the Internet, and they are plenty mad that they still have to interact with the hustlers in the showroom. These consumers are doing their best to turn car dealerships into little more than warehouses where they finally pick up the cars they may have selected, financed, bought, and insured in cyberspace.

Before the advent of the Internet, many other industries as well—insurance, securities brokerage, travel—distributed their products largely through high-cost, high-pressure commissioned salespeople. The argument for these salespeople was that the products were too complex for consumers to buy themselves, so they needed to be "sold." And the success of these middlemen depended on two things: First, the willingness of the brands they represented to give consumers no other way of buying; and second, the ignorance of consumers as to what the options really were and how much their services were costing them.

The first condition, the willingness of brands to restrict their distribution to commissioned salespeople, is now disappearing. The Internet has made one rule clear: Sell the way consumers want or someone else will. Even Merrill Lynch, ground zero for the old-style, full-service stockbroker, has seen the writing on the wall and is allowing its customers to trade securities online.

The second condition that propped up these highly personalized means of distribution is also disappearing. Thanks to the

Internet, the day of the naïve consumer is over. Increasingly, consumers don't need to be "sold," because they enter every transaction already knowing what they want to buy.

These informed consumers are voting with their computer mice, and many old-world brands are reeling right now from the discovery that the first calculation many consumers make before they buy *anything* is, "Can I get comfortable enough about this product without talking to a salesperson?"

Let's face it: The flight from the commissioned salesperson is happening with good reason. Traditionally, salespeople have been given all the wrong incentives. Generally, because they were owned by one brand, or limited contractually to it, or because one brand paid a higher commission, they would try to narrow your choices. The Chevrolet salesperson, for example, was not about to sell you a Ford, even if it was a better car for you. Even if there were 150 brands available, most salespeople were not capable of learning them all well enough to give you informed advice about them. And since they were paid for completing a transaction, not for keeping you happy long term, they would sell whatever they could sell, whether it was what you needed or not.

It's impossible to spend any time online without thinking of all the transactions in your life that would have gone differently if you'd had more knowledge or better access and hadn't been "assisted" by that salesperson, starting with the crib that your parents bought you when you were six days old. The Internet has caused a mass outbreak of "buyer's remorse"; and whether it's fair or not, the commissioned salespeople of the world are shouldering the blame.

Of course, it's not just the commissioned salesperson who has driven millions of consumers online, but also the salesperson at the opposite end of the spectrum, the hourly wageworker. I first saw this flight from the "customer service representative" as a consumer phenomenon in the 1970s when the banks installed their first Automatic Teller Machines. They expected people to use them mostly after-hours. As soon as the machines went in, of course, the lines to use them were snaking around the block, even during banking hours. Meanwhile, bored tellers stood inside at the counter twiddling their thumbs. The banks were shocked to learn that, given a choice, people preferred to deal with a machine.

Of course, consumers aren't stupid. A machine is usually less likely to raise their blood pressure. "Customer service" may be a mantra in American business, but too many businesses give their employees no incentive to offer it, paying them strictly for the hours they clock, not for the number of customers they knock themselves out to please. Who hasn't had the experience of trying to flag a salesclerk who has perfected the ability not to see customers? To borrow a phrase from Muhammad Ali, they have learned how to practice "the rope a dope." This is the technique Ali used to win against George Foreman in Zaire in 1974. He just stayed on the ropes and let Foreman hit him until Foreman got tired, and then Ali knocked Foreman out. Some salesclerks do their best to tire you out until you give up and go away.

The truth is, a lot of businesses act as if consumers are as plentiful as grains of sand on a beach; and if a few thousand fall through their fingers never to return, well, there are always more. There's only one problem with this attitude: If you make life difficult enough for enough people, you will lose not just those particular customers, but your entire reputation. You do damage to your brand that may be very difficult to recover from.

Clearly waiting for a fall are some of the superstore brands. They may have big selections and good prices, but entering one of them is like entering the Twilight Zone. You're far more likely to find Rod Serling than you are to find someone who can actually assist you. The stores are often extraordinarily messy. The merchandise is stacked so high you often can't get your hands on it without a clerk, but the clerks tend to be scarce. Even if you can find a clerk to talk to you, only 1 out of 10 will know the answer to your questions. Finally, these stores always seem to be short of cashiers; so just when your patience is entirely shot, it takes forever to escape the place.

Consumers will only take this kind of punishment so long as they have no other choices—and, generally, there is always a superior distributor waiting in the wings, eager for the chance to take their business away.

SMART BRANDS DO NOT FRUSTRATE THEIR CUSTOMERS

Imagine arriving in a city and saying to the front desk clerk at your hotel, "You know, I'd like a Coke. Is there someplace here I can get one?" Now imagine hearing back, "Yeah, the guy who sells Coke is down by the marina. You'll have to take a cab."

How likely would you be to pursue that Coke if it meant half an hour roundtrip? Not very likely, right? Coca-Cola knows this, and distributes its brand so widely that in most cities, you won't have to travel more than 100 yards to get your hands on a Coke. Of course, if you buy it in a supermarket, it may cost you 35 cents for 12 ounces; and if you buy it in a fancy restaurant, it may cost you $3.50; but Coke is willing to leave that choice up to you.

Increasingly, smart brands ranging from Charles Schwab to Staples to the Gap are following the Coke formula, allowing the consumer to decide how, where, and when to obtain their products.

At John Hancock, we'd decided by the early 1990s that it made no sense to deny people the ability to shop the way they wanted to shop. Like most of our competitors back then, we did almost all our business through our own proprietary insurance agents. But it was becoming clear to us that this single distribution channel could not possibly answer the needs and desires of all potential John Hancock customers. So we decided for the first time that, instead of making the customers come to us, we'd go to them. Wherever they wanted to buy life insurance, we'd be there.

We began offering Hancock's products through banks, insurance brokers, stockbrokers, financial planners, and the ultra high-end insurance producer M-Group. We also began selling directly over the phone and the Internet, as well as through online aggregators such as Quicken and Quotesmith. The change was radical. In 1991, 5,000 life insurance agents sold John Hancock products. In 2000, 66,000 financial professionals of all shapes and stripes did.

Of course, diversifying our distribution this aggressively meant that we were forced to face up to a problem myriad businesses, from record companies to automakers, are now wrestling with, thanks to the Internet. The polite name for it is "channel conflict." Less politely, it is the wrath of your old bricks-and-mortar distributors, who think that if you give your products to nontraditional distributors, you are supporting their competitors, and if, God forbid, you decide to sell directly to the public, *you* are now the competition.

Initially, John Hancock heard the same arguments many other businesses are hearing today from their old-world distributors: "People will never buy without the human touch." And we heard the same threats: "We'll never sell for you again."

We went ahead anyway. We convinced John Hancock's agents that frustrating consumers who wanted to buy our brand through other channels in no way benefited the agents, but that a stronger company with rising sales would.

Then, we began remaking our agency force into the kind of modern distributor consumers would value. We made them more independent and allowed them to sell other brands of products. And we've encouraged our agents to increase their expertise as financial advisors. The great lesson of the Internet revolution is not that people *never* want personal service, just that they won't pay for personal service that does not add real value to the transaction.

Diversifying Hancock's distribution was clearly the right call. If we had continued to sell our products just through agents, our life insurance and long-term care insurance sales would have declined 20 percent between 1991 and 1999. Because of the growth of our alternative channels, our life and long-term care sales nearly doubled during this period. Since 1991, Hancock's life insurance sales have grown at five times the industry rate.

Do all you can to allow your old-style distributors to succeed, but do not allow them to hold your brand hostage.

Of course, there are instances when limiting your distribution may make sense—if, for example, you are Tiffany & Co., and your success depends on the air of exclusivity attached to your products. For a while, the toy company Ty managed to create an aura of value around something essentially valueless—its Beanie Baby stuffed animals—by restricting their distribution to small specialty stores and releasing them in limited editions.

But unless your products are truly precious and unique, you can only fool people with the haughtiness of your distribution strategy for so long. Today's consumers are demanding the brands they like by any means; and on the whole, it makes very little sense to resist.

FACE UP TO YOUR LIMITATIONS

The Internet is here, and the old-world brands all want to go to the Colosseum to see the games. What some of them don't understand, however, is that they're the contestants. If they fail to do a good job online, they are wounded not just in the virtual world, but also in the stores and offices of the real world. Toys 'R' Us offers an excellent example of how not to compete in today's marketplace—and then, fortunately, how to adjust.

Like many parents of toddlers, I was grateful that Toys 'R' Us had made a big push online in 1999, because it meant that I could do my Christmas shopping at home. To draw people to its website, the company offered several promotions, including the one that hooked me: Spend $100 and get a free Tickle Me Elmo doll. My son loved Tickle Me Elmo, and I thought that sounded like a pretty good deal.

The day after Thanksgiving, I tried to enter the site and got a message that said they were too busy and to try back later. When I finally did get in, I had trouble finding what I was looking for. I entered "Pooh" in the search box. The site couldn't identify any such item. Is it possible, I wondered, that Toys 'R' Us is Pooh-less? No, just clueless. I finally figured out that I needed to type in "Winnie the Pooh and Friends" to get the list of toys I wanted. The problem was, there were only descriptions of some of the toys and only pictures of others, so I couldn't connect them to the television commercials for the particular toy my son wanted. While I was trying to puzzle this out, the website announced, "Your time is up." And they disconnected me! This happened three times.

And my sufferings at the hands of toysrus.com were minor compared with those of the estimated five percent of its on-line Christmas shoppers who were informed on December 21 that the toys the company had promised to deliver by December 25 wouldn't get there. A group of attorneys in Washington State actually initiated a class-action lawsuit against Toys 'R' Us for ruining so many kids' and parents' Christmases. Good publicity for a toy brand? I don't think so.

In August of 2000, Toys 'R' Us finally faced up to its limitations and married its online toy business to that of Amazon.com. Amazon agreed to take care of all the tricky aspects of online distribution—customer service, order fulfillment, and warehousing—for inventory provided by Toys 'R' Us.

In return, Amazon now has the biggest brand in toy stores to lure consumers to its own site. I suspect we'll be seeing many more such marriages of established brands with technological know-how in the near future.

The truth is, the Internet can be very hard on older brands that choose to move online themselves. Business, unfortunately, does not have a pro draft, and it's hard to draw the cream of the technical crop to old-world firms. You're much more likely to attract the right talent if you have the right high-tech partners. Even a powerhouse like Wal-Mart, for example, brought in the Silicon Valley venture capital firm Accel Partners to help it launch its website and based its online operation in the middle of the high-tech brain trust in Palo Alto, California, rather than in Bentonville, Arkansas, where its headquarters are located.

And clearly, the future of e-commerce will involve more and more of a sensory experience online. You can already take 3-D tours of the cars you're thinking of buying. It's easy to imagine in the not-so-distant future, websites that mimic the experience of test-driving a car. Advancements like this are clearly not going to come from old-world companies, which are generally more concerned with the limits of technology than with pushing the envelope. These advancements are going to come from the best pure-technology players. What the smart old-world brands will do is make sure they are aligned with those players.

In 1999, John Hancock faced a key decision: Spend $100 million upgrading johnhancock.com as an e-commerce site or partner with the online insurance aggregators that have sprung up in recent years and put our capital to other uses. We decided at that point that we would be far better off forming alliances with high-tech partners who would do the selling for us. It has turned out to be a great decision. We are routinely the number-one brand on the biggest insurance aggregator sites, Quicken and Quotesmith. By 2000, we were selling 60 percent of our term-life policies online.

But we haven't limited ourselves to Quicken and Quotesmith. Rather than attempt to be clairvoyant about which sites were likely to survive in the long term, we made deals with as many Internet insurance aggregators as we could. It's a bit like those people who give to all sides in a political race. They don't care which candidate wins; they just want to be covered.

Ultimately, John Hancock realized that its own proprietary website could never compete with the likes of Internet aggregators, because consumers increasingly demand both their choice of brands when they shop and a degree of objectivity when they're presented with those choices. They increasingly prefer financial supermarkets to distribution owned by a single brand, which explains the tremendous success of marketplaces like schwab.com and which is why even a great financial brand like Fidelity, which used to sell just its own mutual funds, now feels obligated to offer more than 300 brands of mutual funds.

When John Hancock decided in the early 1990s that we would no longer restrict our distribution to our own life insurance agents, we had a little insight: We are primarily a manufacturer, not a distributor. We understood that it would be smarter for us to leave the selling to other people and concentrate on what we were good at—developing innovative products, customizing those products for various distributors, and communicating to consumers about our brand.

In this ferociously competitive business landscape, it will be increasingly difficult for many brands to succeed as both manufacturers and distributors. The companies that make up their minds that they are primarily one or the other will find it much easier than the schizophrenics to get their cost structures in place, get their technologies in place, and understand which products to introduce when. Some brands will learn, like Sears has, for example, that they are primarily distributors, not manufacturers, and, therefore, they cannot afford to offer only the house brand of products. And a lot of brands that *were* distributors will discover, like John Hancock, that they are now manufacturers for new distribution media.

BEAT YOUR DISTRIBUTORS INTO SUBMISSION BY CREATING DEMAND FOR YOUR BRAND

The Internet is clearly liberating many brands by loosening the hold old-world distributors have on them. But paradoxically, the Internet is also forcing many brands to cede control over their distribution to new high-tech, third-party players who handle the distribution game better than they ever will. It is incredibly important in this world, however, that manufacturers not cede one thing to their distributors—the care and feeding of the brand.

A strong brand is the only thing that can tip the balance of power between distributors and a manufacturer back into the manufacturer's favor. The contrast between the way distributors handle products with strong brands and the way they handle the products that do not have strong brands could not be more obvious, and the evidence is right there in your local department store.

A rack of Calvin Klein briefs, for example, is never messy. Why? Because of Marky Mark and Antonio Sabato, Jr., and a slew of other high-profile models in a slew of high-profile advertising campaigns.

No, these impressive specimens are not there straightening up, but Klein has used them to create demand for his underwear, and the salespeople follow their customers. The salespeople know that if the Calvin Klein rack is a mess, three things will happen. One, the shoppers who have come to the store specifically to buy Calvin Klein are going to be unhappy, and they will lose commissions. Two, their supervisors will be all over them. Three, if the Calvin Klein rep were to come in, there would be hell to pay. There are no such fears when it comes to the house brand of briefs, so it usually looks like something straight out of a third-world bazaar.

Once you've used your brand to create consumer demand, everything about the manufacturer–distributor relationship is suddenly in your favor. Because your distributors are eager to carry your brand, you no longer have to give them as big a cut of revenues. You can demand commitments from them. You can negotiate better shelf space and in-store promotions.

In 1987, for example, when Martha Stewart first started designing products for Kmart, she could not convince the company to advertise and display her bedding and dinnerware with any zeal. Then, of course, she built herself into one of the great brands of the 1990s. Suddenly, Kmart was moving her goods up to the front of its stores, featuring her in its television commercials, and increasing the number of departments offering her products. She went from begging one Kmart chairman to give her line some support to advising the next chairman on the search for his successor and saying publicly that she'd like a seat on the Kmart board. At this, Kmart tried to put her in her place by saying it avoids having suppliers on its board. But clearly, Stewart is no longer a mere supplier—she is now the one name that sets Kmart apart from the competition. Personally, I would not bet that Stewart doesn't wind up with that seat at some point, thanks to the power of her brand.

With a good brand, you can even force distributors who might not otherwise have carried your brand to do so. The drug companies, for example, have figured out that instead of courting doctors, who no longer have the power and influence they once had, they can sell their prescription products by courting the end-users directly through television and print ads. It doesn't matter that the applications, administration, side effects, indications, and contraindications of these prescription drugs are extremely complex. The drug companies are nonetheless succeeding in turning them into brands, and consumers are demanding them by name. A relentless TV campaign turned the allergy prescription Claritin, for example, into the best-selling product in Schering-Plough history.

The best branding campaigns will work on your distributors in two ways. First, if your brand building campaign is compelling enough to consumers, people will go into stores and ask, "Why don't you carry these products?" All it takes is a few resentful customers to make most distributors afraid *not* to carry your brand. And second, the psychological effects of a strong brand work on distributors just as well as they work on consumers. They will want to sell your brand because they believe it will class up the store, and they will market their association with you as a point of pride.

In a world with an exploding number of distribution options, it is nonetheless easy to come up with a smart distribution strategy if you follow two simple principles: First, sell your products in the ways that your target audience wants to shop; and second, communicate so compellingly to consumers that you make your distributors slaves to your brand.

USE YOUR BRAND TO LEAD YOUR PEOPLE TO THE PROMISED LAND

Whenever I'm asked by an Italian-American, "Where are you from?" I know better than to say, "Utica, New York," the place where I grew up. Instead, I say the village of Gorgoglione, in the province of Matera, in the Basilicata region of Italy, the place my grandparents emigrated from.

Actually, it's rather amazing. Here we are, second- and third-generation Americans—educated, allegedly sophisticated people—identifying each other through the tribal affiliations of people who may have died before we were born, our great-grandparents who spent their lives in ancient hilltop towns that have been rivals with each other for the last eight or nine hundred years, at least.

These rivalries are completely irrelevant to the lives we lead now. Still, we're branded by these villages; and within the larger tribe of Italian-Americans, we use them to comprehend each other and determine a social pecking order. Those of Florentine origin, of course, feel superior to the Romans, who feel superior to the Neapolitans, who, in turn, feel superior to the Sicilians. And this phenomenal attachment to the tribes of one's ancestors is common not just among Italian-Americans, but also among Greek-Americans and Irish-Americans, as well as the Daughters of the American Revolution. The staying power of these ancient affiliations suggests how central brands are to our identity.

Of course, in the larger world, Gorgoglione means very little, and other brands loom large. We are all collections of brands, from the college we attended to whose shoes are on our feet; and the significance of these various brands has shifted radically in the last 50 years. Ethnicity, race, religion, parentage, and hometown matter less and less in America. Even such previous indicators of status as clothes no longer say as much as they used to, thanks to Silicon Valley's unwashed billionaires. More than anything else, your identity in the world at large is determined by what you *accomplish*. This means that the most significant brand any of us bears may very well be the brand of the company we work for. It is one of the prime ways we identify other people, and it is one of the prime components of our own identity.

That is why the first question at any cocktail party is always "What do you do?" And being able to answer with a degree of pride is much more important than most people will admit.

Companies with strong brands therefore have a few enormous advantages in the marketplace:

1. The very best people want to work for them.

2. Their brands help their employees focus and make decisions.

3. Their brands motivate their employees to do more than they otherwise would have believed they could.

Companies with strong brands succeed not just because their brands have such a strong influence on an external audience of consumers, but also because their brands have such a strong influence on an internal audience of employees, vendors, and distributors.

THE BEST PEOPLE WANT TO WORK FOR THE BEST BRANDS

If you ask most people what's most important when they're looking for a job, they'll probably say the following: the pay, the quality of the position they're offered in terms of interest and prestige, and the character of the work environment. But the truth is, the most capable job seekers will probably sacrifice one of these—or all three—for a chance to work for the best brand.

In John Hancock's hometown of Boston, for example, Fidelity Investments is a famously tough place to work, with extremely demanding management; yet it consistently draws the very cream of the crop because it is simply the best brand in its field.

And if the pond is prestigious enough, people are willing not just to put up with demanding bosses, but are also willing to be smaller fishes than they would be someplace else. When I worked at Citibank, for example, the biggest brand in banking, I watched the company attract unbelievable talent. The bench was so deep that people who'd be vice presidents almost anywhere else weren't even officers at Citibank. The company could afford to lose two top people in a division and then, without blinking, replace them the next day with insiders. Good people were just clamoring to be there.

In addition, the best brands generally don't have to pay as much to attract the best people. In a *New York Times Magazine* article titled "0% Unemployment," cultural observer David Brooks took a look at the incredibly tight labor market in Madison, Wisconsin in early 2000. Brooks found that unlike many other companies in the region that had resorted to offering stock options and free maid service to attract new applicants, the top-of-the-line refrigerator brand Sub-Zero had no problem attracting employees and frequently retained them for generations. Brooks concluded, "Again and again, people mention the importance of reputation. . . . Status companies seem to have a big advantage finding workers."

In 2000, *Fortune* magazine did a fascinating comparison. It calculated the average number of job applicants per opening for two groups of companies: those on its list of the "One Hundred Best Companies to Work For" and those on its list of the "Top Ten Most Admired Companies," which included huge brands like Microsoft, Dell, Intel, and Wal-Mart. One list emphasized worker-friendliness, the other marketing and operational prowess.

Guess which group had more applicants per job? The market leaders won out over the companies that bent over backwards to make their employees happy by a margin of two to one—26 applicants per job versus 13.

Of course, job seekers aren't stupid, and they are drawn to the best brands for a number of reasons. One factor is, naturally, status. People are impressed when you say you work for a market leader. Another is the personality of the workplace. Since these companies are able to hire the best talent in the marketplace, they tend to be very dynamic places, nonbureaucratic, and full of new ideas.

And probably most important, the best brands are the best places to be *from*. These names work magic on a résumé, which is, after all, not just a statement of experience, but also a collection of more and less desirable brands that determines your relative desirability as a job seeker.

When people look at a résumé and see that you've worked at Citigroup, Disney, Coca-Cola, or Microsoft, suddenly you're a star. You may not even be a capable person, but the simple fact that you've worked at one of these top-shelf companies may get you the job. If it's a choice between a terrific journalist who works for a regional newspaper and a mediocre reporter who works for the *New York Times*, the *Times* guy will almost always get the job. It's not fair, but it's not entirely wrong to presume that the more capable people will come from the better brand.

Of course, this can be a strange, Faustian bargain for a company with a great brand. You can get the best people to work for you for less money, sometimes in lesser positions; and you can work them very hard—mainly because they want to put your name on a résumé when they leave you.

The truth is, we live in a very mobile work world. It's not necessarily better for their careers if the people you hire stay with you forever. And it's not necessarily better for you to keep them forever either, no matter how good they are while they're with you, because that's how bureaucrats are made. We've tried to create a culture at John Hancock where as important as it is to be *at* the company, it's just as important to be *from* John Hancock—a true test of the quality of the brand. We expect our most talented employees to eventually move on to other things. We just want them to know when they do go that they have come from a great place.

And it is not just the best employees who are drawn to the best brands, but the best distributors as well. Salespeople, of course, all possess the unshakable belief that the value they personally add to the transaction is more important than any other factor in generating a sale, and to some extent, it's true. But they also know very well that it is hard to get in the door if they don't represent a company that has a solid reputation. If you are a great brand, great salespeople will be eager to sell you, reluctant to leave you, and more tolerant of minor annoyances such as slow service.

And the best vendors of all sorts will try their hardest to win your business, because they know your brand will enhance their reputation and draw other big clients. The advantages can be great. If two companies with equal buying power need a printing job done at the same time, the printer is far more likely to accommodate the better brand.

A STRONG BRAND MAKES TOUGH DECISIONS EASIER

Companies with strong brands find that they can do things lesser brands cannot, not just because of the quality of the people they attract, but also because the brand makes decision making so much easier up and down the line.

Let's presume, for example, that your company has to make a decision about product development, such as which product to develop and how much time and money to invest in it.

Naturally, if you are in charge of this process, you'll ask the people who'll be involved with it to tell you which approach they favor. They will all have very strong arguments about how and if it should be done. And they will not agree. Nor will they necessarily tell you what they really think.

Unfortunately, the higher you rise in a corporation, the more people try to conceal the truth from you. They presume that it's politic to flatter you or smart to conceal weaknesses in their own operations. They may not be pathological liars, but they may very well be pathological advocates for their departments or divisions, and a group of them can make it very difficult to discover what reality really is.

The salespeople, for example, always want the product you're developing right away and they want it at a very low price, with as many features as possible, and naturally, the highest possible commission. They'll argue that they can't possibly sell it under any other circumstances, and tell you not to ask them for any commitments. And they very well know they could sell it with fewer features and enough margin to make it profitable, but why should they admit that for a moment?

Meanwhile, the financial people say that you will never make any money on this product unless you charge twice what the salespeople want. The technology people tell you it will take two years before you have systems in place for it and three times more money than you are able or willing to spend. Because the marketing people have to make sure the product has impact in the marketplace, they want millions of dollars to launch it. The product development people tell you the whole thing will be a snap. So you're left wondering, "How could all these people be right?"

The executive's job has a lot in common with Judge Judy's. You sit and listen and people present cases. The difference is, in corporate life, there are never just two sides to the story.

Fortunately, the relative merit of these various points of view suddenly becomes clear once you start to look at them through the prism of your brand. In the case of a product development decision at John Hancock, we'd immediately ask, will this product reflect and enhance our brand? How will we have to market and support it in order to keep this effort consistent with our brand? And the answers start to fall into place.

The truth is, no corporation can afford to be the best at everything, to have the best products, the best technology, the best customer service, the best prices, the best advertising, the best packaging, etc. If you ask yourself, "What do I have to do to support my brand?," the priorities become clear. For Apple Computer, great design is now paramount to the success of the brand. It could afford to produce an awkward mouse, but it could not afford to produce an ordinary-looking computer. For Wal-Mart, great prices are the key; it could not afford to raise its margins significantly. For Tiffany & Co., on the other hand, the quality and uniqueness of the merchandise count most; it could not afford to sell the same cheap flatware as every department store. In the insurance business, ground zero for the brand is processing an insurance claim quickly and delivering it well.

A strong brand can not only set priorities for spending, but can also help you make the truly difficult decisions. If you have a high-quality brand in place that is not to be compromised, it makes many painful questions wonderfully black-and-white, such as whether to fire a problematic employee—even if the employee is somebody you have known for 20 years, somebody who was the best man at your wedding, somebody who makes the company a lot of money. No matter how productive they are, alcoholics, drug addicts, sexual harassers, racists, and hustlers of all types tend to have much shorter half-lives at a market leader than they might at a second-tier company. A great brand stays that way in part because it has no tolerance for anything—or anybody—who threatens the reputation of the enterprise.

And ideally, the brand will make decisions black-and-white not just at the top of the house, but also all the way down the line, so that even the people who answer your phones understand the right way to handle every difficult situation they face. Of course, if you want your employees to express your brand in everything they do, you're going to have to sell your brand to them, too.

A STRONG BRAND WILL INSPIRE THE PEOPLE ON THE INSIDE

Once while in Rome, I went to see some spectacular ancient ruins. It was impossible to look at those three-story columns without imagining the tense job it must have been to raise them. It must have taken hundreds of slaves to pull each one into place. I asked the tour guide, "What happened if one of them fell and broke?"

She said, "Easy. They killed all the slaves."

I suspect that most corporate chieftains would have preferred ancient Rome to the times they live in. But now that slaying the people who work for you is illegal, terror is not quite the motivator it once was. The best way to convince your employees to give you as much as they can is to instill a certain pride in them about the organization they work for and the work they're doing. And while it's very important to motivate your employees as individuals, one of the most effective ways to motivate your workforce as a whole is by building a strong brand.

The people who work for good brands derive a sense of belonging, direction, and purpose from them. This is true even though most people now consider themselves free thinkers, nonconformists, the opposite of those "organization men" of the 1950s who gave their souls to the corporation. But no matter how independent we think we are, we human beings all have an inherent need to belong to something bigger than ourselves. And as other traditional social institutions have faded in importance, the workplace now potentially looms larger as a source of meaning in our lives. People who work for great brands are often inspired by them; and if the brand embodies not just professional excellence, but also certain transcendent qualities such as integrity and empathy, they may do their best to live up to those ideals.

With a great brand, you can convince your employees that they can do things that your competitors' teams can't do, that they can get the products out faster, be more customer focused, be more profitable. That's why army generals bark, "Because we're Americans, we can take that hill." Yes, there is always griping whenever you ask something difficult of your people; but because they really feel dedicated to a greater purpose, they generally deliver. People actually will believe that they can stretch themselves beyond what is possible because they have a great logo on their business card.

The classic example of a brand used extraordinarily well internally, as well as externally, is that of IBM in its heyday in the 1960s and 1970s. Tom Watson Jr. took the best of the devotional culture his father had created at IBM and rethought it for the computer age. By treating his employees well and convincing them they stood for nothing less than excellence, Watson was able to take very ordinary people, put them in white shirts and dark suits, and turn them into an elite corps of the best salespeople in history. He made them believe that because they were part of IBM, they were invincible; and, on that basis, he built one of the great corporations of the 20th century. Sure, IBM had good products, but you know what? Sperry Rand and Control Data had good products, too. What IBM had that these other companies didn't were employees who walked, talked, breathed, and served as the living representations of a very great brand.

A more modern example of something similar is Microsoft. In fact, Microsoft is the odd case of a brand that has worked better on the inside than the outside. Until Judge Thomas Penfield Jackson's antitrust decision gave the company its first recruiting and retention problems, the people on the inside clearly believed that the brand stood for leadership of the entire software industry. On the outside, there has always been the suspicion that the brand has led the industry at least in part because it kneecapped its competitors.

Much of the success of Microsoft is due to the brash, arrogant, but innovative internal culture it has created around its brand. A *Fortune* magazine piece in July 2000 called "I Remember Microsoft" looked at the many young executives who had left the company and gone on to help found new firms. Even in the wake of the antitrust decision, as hard as the reporters tried, they could not get these people to badmouth their alma mater. They all seemed extremely grateful to have come from a place where nothing was impossible. An ex-Microsoftie named Alex St. John, who founded a company called WildTangent, put it this way, "I couldn't be better equipped to run a company. Being CEO is a walk in the park after Microsoft."

Too many companies, however, seem to believe they can achieve this brand effect simply by shouting slogans at their employees. Or by giving them frivolous perks like in-office massages. Or by spending millions of dollars developing a mission statement. Or by presenting a charming face to the people they hope will buy their products, without considering the face they present to the people who make those products. The truth is, it usually takes some work to achieve the corporate equivalent of patriotism. You have to *market* your brand to your employees.

And it is most important to market the brand to those employees who are least likely to benefit by having the brand's name on their résumé—the lower wage workers who are nonetheless most likely to represent the brand in public. While working with a bank client in the late 1970s, I found that the company had done a great job of instilling pride in the executives who worked behind the scenes, but a somewhat poorer job with the only people most of its retail customers would ever meet—its tellers.

I once sat in on a teller training class for this company. The instructor was telling the new hires what to do in the event of a bank robbery. I remember him saying, "If they tell you they have a gun, and you don't see the gun, don't give them the money. If they show you a gun, try to determine if it's real. If you don't think it's real, don't give them the money."

The idea was, you only gave them the money if they came in Patty Hearst style, with a beret and a machine gun.

A very large woman stood up and said, "Let me see if I understand this. You're paying me $4.25 an hour, and you expect me to figure out whether it's a real gun or not? I'll tell you what, some [expletive] walks into the bank and says he has a gun, he's getting ALL the money."

She reconsidered a second, and then said, "You know what? You can keep your job."

I was with her. And I thought it was very, very foolish for a highly regarded bank brand to allow its instructors to act as if the company valued its tellers' lives so little. "We take care of the little guy" was not exactly the message here.

At the other end of the spectrum is a company like Starbucks, which reinforces the cheerful egalitarianism of its coffeehouse experience (the kind of place you'd like to think CEOs and struggling artists meet) by offering every cappuccino maker health insurance, stock options, and a pound of coffee per week.

The choice for brands that employ relatively lowpaid customer service workers is stark. You can either have blue-collar robots as the face of your brand in an increasingly white-collar society, or you can have employees who believe in what they're doing. If you'd prefer the believers to the robots, then "Do as I say, not as I do" doesn't really cut it. You actually have to treat these people in a way that reflects the values projected by your brand.

Every brand builder who hopes to inspire the people who work for him or her will face occasions where he or she is going to have to bite the bullet and actually *live* the brand. John Hancock, for example, had once worked out a deal with a very large affinity group that was going to offer one of our products to its millions of members. This agreement was very important to us. It was potentially worth $50 million in new revenue to us every year, and a lot of very senior people at the company had worked very hard on it. We were just getting down to the final arrangements, when at the last minute the association insisted on taking a bigger cut of the proceeds, making the agreement almost unprofitable for us.

The John Hancock team felt thoroughly misled and used. However, they knew I was friendly with some of the powers that be at the group in question, and they expected me to cave in to their demands.

161

In reality, the decision was easy. We believe the John Hancock brand stands for integrity, and these people had lied to us. There was absolutely no way we were going to put our brand at their mercy. We were out. No negotiation, we were done.

The Hancock people who'd worked on the project actually threw me a surprise dinner to congratulate me for walking away. They saw it as an idealistic decision, but it was thoroughly pragmatic. There was a lot more to be gained by proving to this very valuable group of employees that we really mean the things we say about ourselves than by selling millions of dollars of insurance we could barely make a profit on.

If it's important to reinforce your brand behind the scenes, it's also important to recognize that the things you do out in front of the curtain—advertising, sponsorships, public relations—will register internally as well. The best brand-building efforts are a form of leadership, and they show your internal audience where you want them to go.

At John Hancock, we've deliberately created an image that's out in front of where the organization actually is, and we've used our advertising and sponsorships to help set the standards we'd like our employees to live up to. By the late 1980s, for example, we had been telling our employees for years that we were not a product-push company; instead, we were a company that designed, marketed, and sold its products based on our customers' needs. And for years, it was still business as usual. Then we launched our "Real Life, Real Answers" advertising campaign that said we went out of our way to understand consumers as individuals and to give them the particular products that would serve them best.

162

Suddenly, people inside the company started saying, "Well, we're a needs-based-selling company, we're not a product-push company." Why? Because they saw it on TV. It didn't matter that management had told them a thousand times that's what they were. It wasn't real until they saw it on TV.

Ultimately, you are always speaking to two audiences at once with your brand-building efforts. You can give yourself a ferocious advantage in the marketplace if you make sure that while you're playing the Pied Piper to consumers, you're also using your brand to lead your people to the Promised Land.

10

ULTIMATELY, THE BRAND IS THE CEO'S RESPONSIBILITY—AND EVERYONE ELSE'S, TOO

A brand is more than just advertising and marketing. It is nothing less than everything anyone thinks of when they see your logo or hear your name.

That is why companies that treat their brands as the sole purview of their advertising, marketing, or brand management departments are often unsuccessful. They fail to consider that their brands can be profoundly affected by extensions, acquisitions, distribution, product development, customer service, quality control, etc.—in other words, the entire list of disciplines that it takes to make a business.

And many of the key decisions that determine whether a brand will thrive or fizzle are made when the people whose job it is to be conscious of the brand are not present. That is because many of those decisions are made by lawyers, accountants, salespeople, and software engineers. Often the *only* person in the room looking out for the quality of the brand is the CEO.

This means one thing: The safekeeping of the brand is the CEO's responsibility. The buck stops there.

Unfortunately, many CEOs don't really see it that way. They may feel they have bigger things on their minds. In any given year, most of them will wrestle with dozens of crises that can include inquiries from regulators, products being recalled, even businesses failing. These people are paid well because they're capable of being flexible, of moving from one topic to another, assessing the circumstances, and making a decent decision. And if they're focused on any one thing, they tend to be focused on the financial questions.

Certainly, if you look at what most CEOs emphasize in their own biographies, it's obvious that the skills and accomplishments they cherish most are financial. They highlight the fact that they've grown revenues, made good acquisitions, controlled expenses, and created healthy returns. After all, that's why the shareholders keep them around—to deliver the numbers that drive the stock price up.

I have yet to see a CEO's résumé that says, "Brand expert."

But if a company is going to be successful in the long term, the CEO's first concern has to be the brand. Brand has to trump even short-term financial questions, because all the financial measures, everything from market capitalization to margins, are directly affected by the health of the brand.

A good brand can command a premium price for both its products and its stock. On the other hand, when the brand of an otherwise-successful company has deteriorated, it's like owning a wonderful house in a declining school district. It is only a matter of time before the value of the house goes down dramatically.

CONVINCE YOUR EMPLOYEES TO WORRY ABOUT THE BRAND

The CEOs who don't think of themselves as the caretakers of their brands tend to make a few crucial mistakes.

First, they allow people who don't understand what is at stake to determine the fates of their companies. The Firestone tire scandal of 2000 offers a perfect example of a brand severely damaged by the decisions of employees who probably didn't consider it their job to worry about the brand. According to the *New York Times*, Firestone's financial people knew about the rising number of warranty claims on certain tire models two years before the company finally recalled them. Four years before the recall, the company's engineers were told that vehicles owned by the state of Arizona were experiencing tire failure in hot weather. And over the years, the company's lawyers dealt with a stream of 1,500 legal claims surrounding the problematic tires. Yet, somehow, no one seemed to have informed the safety experts.

If that is all true, the culture of the company was obviously not attuned to the one thing most likely to sink the brand, a perception that Firestone products are unsafe. And clearly, the people at the top were responsible for this failure to make quality control questions the company's first priority. Two months after the recall, Bridgestone-Firestone's chief executive was forced to resign.

At John Hancock, we had our own scandal that could have been nipped in the bud if the right people had blown the whistle early on. The people who processed the paperwork for our sales in the 1980s and early 1990s must have known for years that some of our agents were engaging in inappropriate sales practices, but they failed to tell management.

Since then, however, we've spent a lot of time talking to our employees about how crucial reputation is to the company's success. I'd like to think that our back-of-house people would never look the other way now if they suspected something unethical was going on.

KEEP THE BRAND FRONT AND CENTER IN ALL DECISIONS

The second dire mistake CEOs make is to leave the brand out of those decisions that belong to them and instead to make those decisions based purely on politics, Wall Street, or the bottom line.

The most dramatic examples of decisions that are acutely brand-sensitive, yet not always perceived that way by CEOs, are mergers and acquisitions. And these decisions are being made more and more frequently.

Thanks to the pressure Wall Street puts on public companies for growth and the rising cost of meeting consumers' expectations, consolidation is accelerating in many industries. "Not since the 1890s," reported the *New York Times* in late 2000, "have mergers so extensively concentrated corporate market power." And naturally, if the investment bankers get their way, the mergers—and the fees associated with them—won't stop until there is just one giant company left in the world.

At the same time as CEOs and investment bankers rush into these deals, there is ample evidence that the stocks of the acquiring companies often perform so poorly that the companies would have been better off taking their shareholders' money to Vegas.

One of the big problems with mergers—and the reason they so often deliver such a low return on investment—is that the financials of the deals generally fail to reflect any branding strategy. In other words, most mergers assume that two plus two equals four. But depending on the way the brands of the companies involved are combined, two plus two might equal two, or it might equal six.

Sometimes, the revenue of the combined company will be greater if the more powerful brand swallows the weaker one. Sometimes, it won't be. If the acquired business is too different from the acquiring business, sometimes the dominant brand message won't stretch far enough to cover it. Sometimes, even if the two companies are in the same line of business, revenues will be higher if both brands retain their own identities. Consumers may be willing to absorb only so much of one brand, and stores may be willing to offer only a limited amount of shelf space for it.

The 1986 marriage of mainframe computer manufacturers Sperry and Burroughs is a good example of a merger that, thanks in part to a flawed branding strategy, proved two plus two sometimes equals two. Even though Burroughs subsumed Sperry in what began as a hostile takeover, Burroughs did not tattoo its name on the new acquisition. Instead, a friendlier solution was devised. A contest was held to see which of the employees of the combined company could come up with the best new name. As a result, two great American brands were thrown out the window in favor of a new brand that had to be built from scratch in a highly competitive marketplace. The new company was called Unisys—now, there's a name that trips off the tongue! Not coincidentally, Unisys started shrinking almost the moment it was born.

Clearly, excessive good manners can undermine a merger, but so can raw aggression. Unfortunately, the conquerors in an acquisition often cannot resist behaving like conquerors. When I worked at Commercial Credit, for example, we bought ERA, one of the largest real estate companies in the country. We were a consumer finance company—what did we know about residential real estate? But what we did know was that we wanted to put our name on the business. So years were spent trying to slap ERA into our advertising programs and assert the dominance of the Commercial Credit brand, diminishing ERA in consumers' eyes in the process. This happens more frequently than you would think: A corporation pays dearly to acquire an existing brand, only to do everything possible to destroy its value.

Contrast this high-testosterone behavior with that of a truly brilliant businessperson, Sandy Weill of Citigroup. Every time he has acquired a company with a better brand than the one he had, he has made that the dominant brand of his business. With Weill in charge, Commercial Credit shed its egotistical fixation on its own name. When it bought Primerica, it humbly became Primerica. When Primerica merged with Travelers, an even better brand, it became Travelers; and when Travelers merged with Citicorp, it became Citigroup, the best brand of them all.

By definition, mergers involve cultural struggle. As these mergers increasingly cross international lines (e.g., Equitable becomes AXA Financial and Chrysler becomes DaimlerChrysler); and as these mergers link new-economy brands with powerful old-economy brands (e.g., AOL buys Time Warner), the struggles are only going to become more difficult to manage.

Many corporations will find themselves puzzling over the value of the various brand messages in their stables. Do you allow one brand to overtake another? Is the dominant brand elastic enough to cover the acquired business? When a brand that's big in France, but unknown in America, buys a big American brand, which name do you use? Should you keep two separate brands? Or do you shed both brands and form something new?

Usually, however, when you get down to the final talks with the other side in a potential merger, the question of whether the executives' cars are going to be Mercedes or Cadillacs gets as much attention as what the name of the company will be.

There is no one right answer to the question of which brand or brands should rule in a merger. But it is nonetheless a crucial decision, and the way it is made should have nothing to do with internal politics. Pleasing consumers should be the CEO's only consideration. The brands that survive should be the ones that are most meaningful to consumers.

DO NOT FORGET WHAT THE BRAND MEANS

The final great mistake made by senior executives who don't consider the brand their primary job is to lose sight of what the brand means and to lose their grip on their companies in the process.

One of my alma maters offers a good example. Control Data, portions of which still survive under a different name, was once a computer giant that was a rival to IBM. It was a great company full of brilliant people, including founder William Norris and legendary supercomputer designer Seymour Cray. The company was extremely successful in the 1960s and 1970s selling advanced computers to the government and industry.

Then came the race riots of the summer of 1967, which deeply affected the company's socially minded management. They decided that Control Data would use technology to meet society's unmet needs.

Unfortunately, however, Control Data's civic activities were not restricted to the garden-variety corporate philanthropy—write the check, pose for the pictures, go home. They were about actually remaking Control Data's business mix to include socially useful ventures in fields the company knew little about.

For example, the company spent nearly a billion dollars—many years' worth of operating profits from its computer divisions—creating PLATO, an interactive educational system designed to run on Control Data's mainframe computers. The problem was, the traditional education market couldn't afford the expensive hardware and connections PLATO required.

Another program, dubbed "cars for cons" by the press, was launched when the company discovered that people getting out of prison had trouble holding down jobs because they didn't have transportation to get to them. So the company decided to lease them used cars cheaply. The ex-convicts—surprise, surprise—stole 34 cars, and Control Data became a laughingstock.

Control Data also decided it would meet society's needs by bartering with the technology-deficient nations of the world. It sent millions of dollars' worth of computers to China and the Soviet Bloc countries in exchange for junk like Russian-made Christmas cards and Yugoslavian wine. This meant that the company was constantly distracted by the struggle to unload stuff that had nothing to do with the computer business, including my favorite, cases and cases of Soviet shotguns.

The shotguns, actually, were pretty good guns, but almost worthless in the marketplace, since it was virtually impossible to get parts for them. In addition, the Soviets had just invaded Afghanistan, which did not add to their popularity. Control Data had umpteen guns to dispose of, so it started advertising in the cafeteria its willingness to sell them to employees. You know, your confidence in the company you work for starts to erode a bit when they start hawking Soviet shotguns—cheap—in the cafeteria.

Little by little, these follies chipped away at the once-mighty Control Data brand.

The official history of Control Data's successor captures the problem perfectly. It recounts Control Data's expansion into businesses designed to provide services to the disadvantaged and then states, "By the early 1980s, Control Data perhaps was best known by many people for these small businesses, although computers and peripheral equipment accounted for the vast majority of the Company's revenues."

In other words, the brand message was now on one side of the room, and the businesses that nourished the company were on the other. Schizophrenia like this is untenable, because people follow the brand. What's left behind will inevitably atrophy.

A lot of people believe that because the leaders of Control Data said the brand was all about meeting society's unmet needs, the company began to neglect the base business, the mother lode, the goose that laid the golden eggs. Resources that should have helped Control Data keep up in the ferociously competitive technology marketplace were frittered away. Control Data began to be seen as no longer cutting edge. Eventually, a large and powerful company became a smaller and more marginal one.

A HEALTHY RESPECT FOR THE BRAND IS CONTAGIOUS

If an entire corporation tends to go astray when the CEO loses sight of the brand, the opposite tends to happen when the CEO focuses on it. Suddenly, everybody up and down the line becomes a brand expert. The financial people start considering more than revenues when faced with a potential acquisition. They start worrying about something very unusual, the acquisition target's reputation.

The company's lawyers start developing a peculiar taste for honesty over stonewalling in the company's communications.

The company's advertising people start having the courage of their convictions and refuse to let nonpros—no matter how high up they are in the corporate hierarchy—interfere in the process of producing the advertising.

The information technology people start thinking a little less like engineers and a lot more like marketers, and make sure they offer the company's customers a technological interface that does the brand credit.

The clerks processing the sales become attuned to anything the least bit fishy and alert management to it, because they know their brand stands for integrity.

When the CEO says the brand comes first, employees up and down the line start taking a broader view and feeling responsible for the brand in their own work. The cumulative result can be a truly powerful advantage in the marketplace: 1,000 or 10,000 people, each adding value to the brand every day.

Companies that become great brands do not do so solely by riding the coattails of a few brilliant television commercials. They become great brands because every contact the consumer has with that company, from calling a toll-free information number to actually lacing up the product and using it, is seamlessly enjoyable.

This only happens when everybody from design to shipping becomes an expert on the care and feeding of the brand. And that only happens when the CEO convinces them that no matter what they do, the brand is the most important part of the job.

GOOD BEEF VERSUS BAD

When I was a little boy, my family owned a grocery store in Utica, New York. Dealing with our suppliers was often tricky. Supermarkets were coming into fashion; and because we were a small shop, we had comparatively little leverage. Our meat supplier, in particular, was a problem. They would sell the best meat to the supermarket and then try to pawn off the stuff going bad onto small operations like ours.

To keep them from getting away with this, we didn't just order our supplies on the phone. We would go to the meat packing plant twice a week ourselves to pick out our order. Of course, the meat lockers were so cold, you simply couldn't smell which carcasses were going bad, but my grandmother had this very useful ability. She could actually taste the bacteria on a bad piece of meat. It made her tongue tingle.

Genetically, I drew the short straw, because I had the very same ability. So when my grandmother grew too old and frail to make the trip to the slaughterhouse, my grandfather took me. I was only about four or five years old, but I'd get up twice a week at five in the morning in order to go lick pork butts, two sides of beef, a lamb. A guy in a white coat would point to a side of beef and I would go test it and, as often as not, shake my head no. As you can imagine, the men in the white coats hated me. They used to call me "the licking brat."

My grandfather brought his own "D'Alessandro Store" brand stamp with him. When I approved of a piece of meat, he would stamp it, so the supplier couldn't switch the meat later. And at the end of the "licking session," I would get a reward—a warm hotdog, freshly made, shot out of one of their machines.

Believe it or not, I've often thought that was good training for corporate life. The brand stamp winds up on everything a corporation does. And an executive has to consider, with every move, whether he or she is putting that stamp on something rotten or something sound. Sometimes, there is ample evidence one way or the other. Often, however, it's only instinct that will guide you to the right answer.

What is truly important is asking the question.

"Will it help or hurt the brand?" is the most useful of all mantras in the marketplace. It is the prism through which every business decision, major or minor, can and should be made.

A business focused this way on the quality of the brand is a business that understands the importance of pleasing its employees, stockholders, customers present and future, board of directors, regulators, and potential merger partners—in other words, the audiences that decide a company's fate.

In a world of commerce that often seems to invite egomania and navel gazing, a brand-based business looks outward and is often a jump ahead of the less brand-based competition because of it.

And far from wasting its money and talent on airy concerns, it is, on the contrary, determinedly fixed on the most significant of all bread-and-butter issues: Do people respect our company enough to buy from us?

A business focused on its brand is, very simply, a business primed for success.

INDEX